BEYOND SURFACE CURRICULUM

CURRICULUM

AN INTERVIEW STUDY OF TEACHERS' UNDERSTANDINGS

Published in 1976 in the United States of America by

Westview Press, Inc.
1898 Flatiron Court
Boulder, Colorado 80301
Frederick A. Praeger, Publisher and Editorial Director

Library of Congress Cataloging in Publication Data

Bussis, Anne M.
    Beyond surface curriculum.

    Bibliography: p.
    1. Teaching. 2. Learning, Psychology of.
3. Teachers--Attitudes. 4. Open plan schools.
I. Chittenden, Edward A., joint author. II. Ama-
rel, Marianne, joint author. III. Educational
Testing Service. Early Education Group. IV. Ti-
tle.
LB1025.2.B87   372.1'1'02   75-31640
ISBN 0-89158-014-X

Printed and bound in the United States of America.

The authors wish to thank the following copyright holders for
the privilege of quoting from their works:

Academic Press Inc.: for the excerpt from "Brief Introduction to Personal
Construct Theory" by G. A. Kelly in *Perspectives in Personal Construct
Theory* edited by D. Bannister. Copyright © 1970. Reprinted by permis-
sion of Academic Press Inc.

Agathon Press: for the excerpt from "An Evaluation of Evaluation" by
J. B. Macdonald in *The Urban Review*, Vol. 7, 1974, p. 9. Reprinted by
permission of Agathon Press.

BEYOND SURFACE CURRICULUM

AN INTERVIEW STUDY OF TEACHERS' UNDERSTANDINGS

Anne M. Bussis
Edward A. Chittenden
Marianne Amarel

WESTVIEW PRESS•BOULDER, COLORADO

Allyn & Bacon, Inc.: for the excerpt from *The Culture of the School and the Problem of Change* by S. B. Sarason. Copyright © 1971. Reprinted by permission of Allyn & Bacon, Inc.

American Educational Research Association: for the excerpt from "Curriculum: State of the Field" by John I. Goodlad in the *Review of Educational Research,* Vol. 39, Summer 1969, p. 369 and for the excerpt from "Curriculum Materials" by W. James Popham in the *Review of Educational Research,* Summer 1969, p. 320. Copyright 1973, American Educational Research Association, Washington, D. C. Reprinted by permission.

The American Scholar: for the excerpt from "The Despairing Optimist" by René Dubos in *The American Scholar.* Reprinted from *The American Scholar,* Vol. 41(4), Autumn 1972. Copyright © 1972 by the United Chapters of Phi Beta Kappa. By permission of the publishers.

Education Development Center, Inc.: for the excerpt from "A Plan for Continuing Growth" by D. E. Armington, 1968, and for the excerpt from "Conditions for Growth, Unpublished Working Paper of Follow Through Program" by Education Development Center, Inc., 1972. Reprinted by permission of the Education Development Center.

David Hawkins: for the excerpt from *The Informed Vision: Essays on Learning and Human Nature,* Agathon Press, 1974, and for the excerpt from an informal talk presented at the Advisory for Open Education, Cambridge, Massachusetts, 1973. Reprinted by permission of David Hawkins.

Ann C. Hazlewood and Martha A. Norris: for the excerpt from "The Open Corridor Program: An Introduction for Parents," 1971. Reprinted by permission of the authors.

Hodder & Stoughton Educational: for the excerpt from *The Children We Teach* by Susan Isaacs. Copyright © 1965 (2nd (reset) edition). Reprinted by permission of Hodder & Stoughton Ltd.

Johns Hopkins University Press: for the excerpt from *Mind: An Essay on Human Feeling, Volume I* by Susanne Langer. Copyright © 1967. Reprinted by permission of Johns Hopkins University Press.

Jossey-Bass, Inc.: for the excerpt from "Profession Anyone?" by H. A. Thelen, in *New Perspectives on Teacher Education* edited by D. J. McCarty. Reprinted by permission of Jossey-Bass, Inc.

The Journal of Educational Research: for the excerpt from "What Good Teaching Is" by J. A. Zahorik in *The Journal of Educational Research,* Vol. 66, 1973, p. 439. Reprinted by permission of *The Journal of Educational Research.*

Macmillan Publishing Co., Inc.: for the excerpt from "The Balance of Control and Autonomy in Elementary School Teaching" by D. C. Lortie in *The Semi-Professions and Their Organization,* edited by A. Etzioni, copyright © 1969 by The Free Press, a Division of Macmillan Publishing Co., Inc.; and for the excerpt from *The "Why" of Man's Experience,* by Hadley Cantril, copyright © 1950. Reprinted by permission of Macmillan Publishing Co., Inc.

CONTENTS

                                                                    Page

Acknowledgments   viii

Introduction   1

Chapter 1   A Framework for Educational Research   7

        2   Open Education and Teacher Development   21

        3   Description of the Study   33

        4   Teachers' Understandings of Curriculum   49

        5   Teachers' Understandings of Children   79

        6   Phenomenological Inquiry   113

        7   The Working Environment of the School   123

        8   Teachers' Perceptions of Support from
             Advisors   137

Postscript   The Interview in Retrospect   169

References   173

Appendix 1   The Teacher Interview   179

Appendix 2   Curriculum Priorities Coding   191

ACKNOWLEDGMENTS

The Ford Foundation provided major financial support for the research reported in this book, and Educational Testing Service funded the initial planning and final writing stages of the project. Neither the research nor the book would have been possible, however, were it not for the insights, constructive criticism, cooperation, and kindnesses of many people. We trust that each of the following persons already knows our appreciation.

Sue Burkhart, Helen Neuberg, Masako Tanaka, Nancy White, and Barbara Vilkomerson	Formerly with Educational Testing Service
Dale Bussis	Formerly with the Institute for Educational Development
Lilian Katz	University of Illinois
Marjorie Martus	The Ford Foundation
Samuel Messick	Educational Testing Service
William Meyer	Syracuse University
Patricia Carini and colleagues	The Prospect School
Vito Perrone (and members of the Study Group on Evaluation)	University of North Dakota
Ann Cook, Herb Mack, and staff	Community Resources Institute
George Hein and David Armington	Formerly with the Follow Through Program, Education Development Center
The Follow Through staff, both central and local	Education Development Center; Burlington, Vermont; and Scranton, Pennsylvania
Floyd Page and staff	Creative Teaching Workshop
Lillian Weber and staff	The Open Corridor Program and The Workshop Center for Open Education

Edward Yeomans and staff Greater Boston Teachers
Center

Miriam Godshalk, editor for the Developmental Research Division
at ETS, has contributed much time and talent to this book. She
not only critiqued and edited the draft manuscript, she oversaw
all the final operations necessary in preparing the copy for publication.

We also acknowledge the important contributions of **Nora Kim,**
especially during the long coding phase of the study. Although
coding was an interesting task, it was an arduous and demand-
ing one. The entire coding and data analysis process was greatly
strengthened by her efforts.

We are grateful, too, to **Lillian Weber** for support and critical
analysis of our work. We have gained much from her substantive views about teacher development; and, in general, her perspectives have helped clarify our own.

A special note of gratitude is reserved for **Joan Tamburrini** of
the Froebel Institute, London, who helped immeasurably in
thinking through complex aspects of the research. In fact, at
this point in time it is virtually impossible to sort out who
originated what ideas, particularly with respect to several of the
coding schemes. She is a valued colleague and friend.

Sixty other people—**the teachers**—were also colleagues in this
study. Their thoughtful comments and responses to the interview reflect a richly varied spectrum of viewpoints and understandings about what it means to teach. We learned a great
deal from the teachers, for which we are deeply indebted. We
are also indebted to them for much of the material that appears
in this book, as we have paraphrased illustrative comments
from over half of the interviews. We hope to thank all of the
teachers in expressing our appreciation to four who gave us
permission to quote them at length and who reviewed parts of
the draft manuscript: **Geraldine Charney, Ann Chase, Ileen
Schoenfeld,** and **Michael Trazoff.**

A.M.B.
E.A.C.
M.A.

INTRODUCTION

This book is based on an in-depth interview with 60 teachers who, in 1972, were associated with an advisory program or a teacher center sponsoring an "open education" approach to instruction. The purpose of the study has been to investigate the understandings and constructs of these teachers for reasons that can best be described as *theoretical, methodological,* and *practical.*

Theoretically, the work of the Early Education Group at ETS has been characterized by a developmental view of the child, an interactive view of learning, and a person-oriented view of human functioning. The interactive and person-oriented viewpoints (formally called a neo-phenomenological position) are examined in Chapter 1. It is sufficient to say here that this position assumes that internal mental processes (such as understandings, beliefs, and values) are major underlying determinants of behavior and of the environments that people create. Translated to teaching, this means that the most significant educational variation exists at the level of the individual practitioner—not at the level of instructional materials, packaged programs, or the like. Although materials and special programs or equipment obviously can be valuable, their value in the long run is determined by the teacher's interpretation and use of them. Given this theoretical position, it becomes clear that teachers' thinking is a critical matter for research. Maxine Greene (1973) argues a similar rationale from the vantage point of the individual educator:

1

There are no final answers, nor are there directives to govern every teaching situation. If he is to be effective, the teacher cannot function automatically or according to a set of predetermined rules. Teaching is purposeful action. . . .

[The teacher's] intentions will inevitably be affected by the assumptions he makes regarding human nature and human possibility. Many of these assumptions are hidden; most have never been articulated. If he is to achieve clarity and full consciousness, the teacher must attempt to make such assumptions explicit; for only then can they be examined, analyzed, and understood. (pp. 69-70)

The theoretical bias we hold is also consonant with a line of philosophy that has influenced educational thought and practice for at least the past two centuries. From Froebel's kindergarten through Dewey's progressive school to the open education movement of today, there lies a basic continuity of assumptions about teaching and learning. The assumptions, of course, have become more sophisticated as they have been increasingly informed by work in related disciplines. Contemporary expressions of this philosophy emphasize the central role of both teacher and child in decisions that determine the nature and course of learning. Unlike other conceptions of instruction in which the teacher's decisions are based largely on criteria and information external to individual children, open education clearly espouses an interactive view of teaching and learning. Because of these many theoretical congruences, research on the understandings of practitioners working in open classrooms was a logical undertaking.

Our methodological objectives in undertaking the study were relatively simple. We hoped to explore the usefulness of an in-depth interview for eliciting internalized assumptions and constructs about teaching. A rationale for the interview technique is given in the beginning chapter of the book, and tentative conclusions about this methodology and the coding schemes it entailed are presented in the Postscript.

Practical reasons for initiating the study may be summarized as the need for more information relevant to teaching practice. Although interesting accounts of open classrooms exist in the literature, their point of departure is frequently the highly-experienced practitioner. It seemed important, therefore, to gain a better understanding of the constraints, problems, and supports that teachers perceive in their beginning years of "opening up."

2

The book falls short of achieving this objective in a systematic fashion, as its major emphasis is on a theoretical analysis of teachers' understandings. Nonetheless, the many interview excerpts that are presented capture insights, skepticisms, enthusiasms, and frustrations that are likely to accompany any teacher's efforts to change in a more open direction.

Chapter 1 discusses problems inherent in behavioral and psychometric approaches to educational research, and questions the adequacy of this contemporary paradigm as a theoretical framework for looking at schools. It suggests an alternative, neo-phenomenological framework derived from the phenomenological argument in philosophy and from convergent theory within the realms of clinical practice, developmental psychology, and psycholinguistics. Methodological implications of the framework are considered in a beginning attempt to outline a paradigm more intrinsically related to the realities of teaching and learning. Discussion also focuses on the role of values in evaluation and research.

Chapter 2 attempts to articulate some key assumptions of the open education position, as we have interpreted these from the literature and from a close association with educators over a number of years. In particular, the chapter focuses on assumptions regarding the teacher as a central decision-maker. It goes on to analyze a conception of in-service support that is viewed as critical for the teacher's continuing growth and development in such a role. In discussing some of the philosophical and theoretical underpinnings of open education, this chapter also provides a kind of general rationale for many of the coding schemes presented in subsequent sections of the book.

Chapter 3 is devoted to a description of the study. In a somewhat cursory fashion, it covers four basic components: (1) the advisory programs and teacher centers with which the teachers in the study were associated; (2) the teacher population and how the interviews were conducted; (3) how the interview was developed; and (4) the development of coding schemes and the coding process. In characterizing this chapter as cursory, we are especially aware of the last two components. The chapter is not intended as a manual on interview construction, nor does it (or the entire book) begin to fulfill requirements necessary for anyone interested in using the coding procedures as we used them. The latter requirements call for a detailed technical manual that would be a major undertaking in and of itself. Although we do not anticipate writing such a manual in the foreseeable future, we have upon occasion worked with others to explain and demonstrate the coding process.

Chapter 4 begins a discussion of results derived from the study, starting with an analysis of teachers' understandings of curriculum. A distinction is drawn between the surface content of curriculum and a deeper level of organizing content—with "surface" referring to the manifest activities and materials in a classroom and the "deeper level" referring to the purposes and priorities a teacher holds for children's learning. Analysis is also made of the relationship between teachers' curriculum constructs and the values they perceive in different kinds of instructional material. It should be noted that these analyses center on variables other than substantive knowledge of subject matter. Thus, the chapter presents only a partial picture of curricular understanding, but it is a part that has been seriously neglected in past research.

Chapters 5 and 6 focus on differing conceptions of children's resources for learning. The first of these chapters analyzes the instructional significance teachers perceive in a child's emotions, interests, capability of choice, and social interactions. Chapter 6 introduces the concept of phenomenological inquiry in attempting to integrate the results discussed in Chapter 5.

Chapters 7 and 8 take up the teachers' views of the support they were receiving in their professional development. Support within the institutional resources of the school is analyzed from global ratings of the interview. A more detailed treatment is given to perceptions of support from external advisors in the Advisory Programs.

In a postscript, we discuss the interview and interview methodology in retrospect. We briefly describe other studies that have utilized the present interview and coding schemes (or some modified version of them) and indicate what tentatively appear to be generalizable features of the overall methodology.

It is obvious that this study addresses only one piece of an overall puzzle surrounding the nature and import of teachers' understandings. There need to be more studies of what we have attempted to investigate, to say nothing of research directed to situational and contextual influences on decision-making, the origins of teacher constructs, and, of ultimate importance, the

4

differential and interactive effects that teachers' understandings have upon children's learning.

We have sometimes been asked where a particular coding scheme "comes from." This question invariably concerns a theoretical coding scheme rather than an empirically-derived one, and it is a difficult question to answer. An easy answer, of course, is that the coding schemes "come from" our heads, but that is hardly the whole story. Basically, they represent a synthesis of our own theoretical predilections with what we have come to understand about the aims of open education—aims that constitute a directional heading rather than a destination to be "arrived at." The more important distinction to be made about most of the theoretical coding schemes is that they are multidimensional. That is, some categories of a scheme are intended to reflect psychologically equivalent or similar expressions of a particular aim of open education; other categories reflect qualitatively different aims rather than quantitative deviations from the intended aim.

Another question that has arisen concerns differences between programs or sites in the study. Since we thought that program comparisons were premature and deliberately ruled them out of the analysis, this question will not be answered by reference to specific data. We can say, however, that variation across a wide range of perceptions and understandings about curriculum and children existed at all sites.

Finally, the reader may well wonder about the degree of integration and consistency within teachers' understandings. We have touched on this issue in some analyses, but admittedly have not carried it through to a logically satisfying completion. There appears to be considerable consistency within teachers' construct systems; the problem lies in how to interpret and present this consistency. Although we did not exhaust the interview data (they are virtually inexhaustible), we did perform many more analyses than appear in the following chapters. It was the conceptual complexity of these analyses that dictated against our including them in the book.

In summary, the intent of this book is a provocative one. We do not claim a comprehensive coverage of the several issues involved. The analyses and speculations made here are for the purpose of sharing what is now available in the hope that it will stimulate alternative approaches to research and will strengthen a growing trend in American education that clearly recognizes the centrality of the teacher's role.

5

CHAPTER
1
A FRAMEWORK FOR EDUCATIONAL RESEARCH

Impetus for change in educational evaluation and research is gathering strength from several sources. Within the field of teaching practice, many leading spokesmen have provided stimulation by directing educational debate away from questions of method to a reconsideration of basic assumptions— assumptions about how children learn, about the teacher's role in curricular and instructional decisions, about the network of human relationships that constitutes a school. Such debate has brought out a number of issues related to evaluation and to the particular assumptions inherent in conventional evaluation methodology.

A second source for change comes from within the evaluation and research field itself. Having made limited contributions to the understanding or improvement of classroom teaching, it is a field now undergoing considerable reappraisal. "What's the matter?" is a question being asked not just by occasional critics, but by acknowledged leaders within the measurement profession. One explanation offered for the apparent impotence of much of the data-gathering activity is insufficient technical sophistication. It is often argued that advances will come with more refined measuring instruments and with more elaborate data-analysis techniques.

7

Without at all minimizing the desirability of better instruments and techniques, we will argue the position that refinement within the existing conceptual framework is not sufficient. It is the rationale underlying present data gathering and analysis—the basic research and evaluation paradigm—that needs rethinking. This is not a new position. It is one that has been stated by a number of investigators[1] in recent years and one that rests on theoretical assumptions and values shared by many educators.

PROBLEMS IN TRADITIONAL METHODOLOGY

Although a thorough analysis of classical research and evaluation design is beyond the scope of this chapter, two critical factors can be isolated that make the design a problem for evaluator and educator alike.

First, traditional methodology assumes that educational programs can be fully prescribed and defined *apart from* the context in which they are to be introduced by a particular teacher and engaged in by a particular group of children. As Macdonald and Clark (1973) point out, such a rationale acts to bypass the processes of instruction and learning by making a direct connection from curriculum to student achievement. This, of course, is reflected in the familiar "educational program ⟶ student outcomes" evaluation design. Even when interaction between children and the prescribed curricular materials and methods is a concern and presumably taken into account (as in computer program branching and behavioral modification programs), it is nonetheless a very limited and *a priori* conception of interaction that considers only the student's manifest behavior.

In short, it is presumed that the important interactions can be predicted in advance and that extraneous influences originating from either the child or the teacher cannot affect the program seriously enough to alter its intended outcomes. In positing this assumption, traditional methodology envisions education as basically a unilateral or unidirectional process.

Certain corollaries stem from this basic postulate. For example, if educational programs are viewed as unilateral influences, then they may also be viewed as exportable. All that has to be done is to find the best method for teaching something and then to implement that method in all classrooms. Another derivative of

[1]See, for example, Carini, 1975; Eisner, 1969, 1971; Jackson, 1970; Macdonald, 1974; Macdonald and Clark, 1973.

8

the unilateral assumption is the emphasis on ensuring uniform implementation of an educational program. Efforts are directed toward honing the teacher's behavior so that certain principles and specific sets of responses will be enacted in systematic fashion. The focus is on decreasing variability between teachers by attempting to standardize their performance.

To date, at least, there is little evidence to support the exportable corollary, and conflicting but mainly negative evidence with respect to whether or not educational programs can be implemented uniformly. Where data do exist that suggest teachers have systematically implemented a program (Beller, 1973), the programs in question tend to be tightly structured, academically oriented, and focused on short-term goals of a highly specific and cognitive nature. As Beller implies, it is precisely on this point that methodological demands for uniformity can run head-on into value questions about the aims of education for young children.

A second and related problem with the traditional paradigm is its narrow conception of operationalism. Educational programs and outcomes are presumed to be optimally stated in concrete, behavioral terms. Since behaviorism and its implications have been argued in the professional literature for years,[2] there is no need to elaborate further here. With respect to the behaviorism that pervades traditional methodology, we would agree with Macdonald (1974) in his predictions of what will happen as we increase control over the educational process through (traditional) evaluation:

> First, we will reduce all significant school-related human behavior to performative acts. In the process, we will say in effect that what takes place internally is either illusory or irrelevant to our concern. . . . We will be in danger of disclaiming any importance to [such an idea as] . . . meaningful behavior may be unobservable and/or internal. (p. 9)

Nowhere is the danger Macdonald fears more evident than in the increasingly specialized and growing field of research devoted to technological curriculum development and "scientific" teaching.

[2]For an unusually thorough and systematic critique of the behaviorist position, see Chein (1972). For a brief but cogent analysis of the philosophical underpinnings of behaviorism and of the constraints these place on educational thinking, see Strike (1974). For a comprehensive description of the contemporary behavior-control teaching model, see Nuthall and Snook (1973).

THE TECHNOLOGICAL RESEARCH EMPHASIS

Before the advent of research specifically aimed at a scientific technology of teaching,[3] the term *curriculum* usually implied the idea of content or subject matter. The word still carries this connotation in common usage today. Over the years, however, educational research has gradually sapped curriculum of its content meaning and injected in its place a "methods" and "form" emphasis. This metamorphosis has been achieved by persistent preoccupation with questions about the formulation and use of educational objectives, the form and organization of curricular materials, and the methods of presenting material.

Such persistence seems unwarranted in light of the repeated empirical finding of no significant differences (with respect to overall measured achievement) between this or that method or between this or that set of materials. From Rice's initial failure to find a best way of teaching spelling up to present day efforts, "no significant differences" is a well-documented phenomenon.[4] As indicated previously, some investigators believe that greater sophistication in evaluation instruments and techniques will eventually yield significant differences. Their belief stems from a faith in measurement technology.

The response of curriculum technologists to the no-significant-differences syndrome carries more serious implications for teaching than the response of the measurement technologists. The former group simply dismisses comparative evaluation studies as irrelevant, partially on the grounds that the programs under investigation do not meet the criteria of an instructional program. Popham (1969) makes the technologists' position explicit.

> Unless one attempts to study replicable curriculum materials, as opposed to those which are essentially unreproducible, it is impossible to attain generalizable results. This conception of curriculum materials as replicable phenomena

[3]Kliebard (1973) places the beginnings of such research around 1895, when Joseph Rice undertook a series of studies to discover the best method of teaching spelling.

[4]See, for example, Stephens, 1967; Kliebard, 1973; Duchastel and Merrill, 1973; Walker and Schaffarzick, 1974.

has great similarity to the conception of an *instructional product,* an *instructional program,* which Markle (1967, p. 104) defined as "a reproducible sequence of instructional events designed to produce a measurable and consistent effect on the behavior of each and every acceptable student." Note that this definition of an instructional program specifies reproducibility both of the instructional *stimuli* and of the *effects* of the student's interaction with those stimuli. (pp. 319-320)

What is extraordinary about this definition is its indifference to the reality of education, because instructional programs that meet these criteria clearly do not exist in present-day schools, nor have they ever existed. In commenting on this type of research, Goodlad (1969) grants the right of investigators to couch research problems in their own terms, but he obviously is worried about it: "If the abstract categories of research and discourse with which [these] scholars deal bear no identifiable relationship to the existential phenomena called curricula, then there is, indeed, cause for concern" (p. 369).

It is not only within the field of curriculum development that a technological approach is becoming firmly rooted. Other attempts to turn teaching into a scientific enterprise come under such guises as a "systems approach" and competency-based teacher education. Since their inception, these and similar movements have been primarily absorbed with the task of defining their own terms and parameters and specifying their particular methods and techniques. This engrossment with definition and method reflects an attempt to develop a science related not so much to crucial problems within its field as to its own refinement—a science that has relevance mainly for the particular research studies it initiates. It is an attempt to develop the procedures of physical science in a vacuum, without addressing the kind of persisting problems that mark the field of education. Susanne Langer (1967) has commented at some length on this tendency within the social sciences. As she points out:

> The main concern of the early physicists was to understand puzzling events; each scientific venture grew from a problem, the solution of which threw unexpected light on other problematical phenomena. . . . But the chief preoccupation of the social scientists has been with the nature of their undertaking. . . . For decades, therefore, the literature of those new disciplines, especially of psychology, has dealt in large

11

measure with so-called "approaches," not to some baffling and challenging facts, but to all the facts at once, the science itself. (pp. 33-34)

The time seems long overdue for research to drop the technological ideal and to take up more direct lines of inquiry into education as it is practiced and experienced by teachers and children in schools.

DIRECTIONS FOR A NEW CONCEPTUALIZATION

Certainly there are many people who have endeavored to understand education and who have been interested in the problems that confront teachers and children in school. But development of an adequate conceptual framework for looking at schools is a difficult task, given the assumptions inherent in traditional methodology. The preceding discussion suggests that construction of a different methodological paradigm must be based on an interactive notion of education and on a view of persons other than that portrayed by behaviorism and technology. Assuming these conditions, however, where does one look for guidelines? In what direction, psychologically speaking, should we move? One alternative is a methodology stemming from the neo-phenomenological tradition in psychology and embracing a number of philosophical and developmental concepts.

The neo-phenomenological tradition[5] in psychology is characterized, first of all, by the assumption that no one can experience a reality that is interpretation-free. We can only make assumptions about reality, construing and interpreting it in terms derived from our individual past histories. At the roots of this tradition is the assertion that man's most distinguishing characteristic is his striving to make sense of experience: to understand it, in whatever terms, in order to make it meaningful, manageable, predictable. Obviously, we come to have some identically shared meanings with others by virtue of widely shared cultural experiences. But most meanings are only partially shared, and in some cases, the overlap is scarcely adequate to permit communication. The meaning of education is an all too

[5]Along with Kelly (1955 a and b), we have chosen to call this a "neo" tradition because the extreme form of phenomenalism and existentialism in philosophy assumes a degree of individual uniqueness that would preclude any meaningful generalizations and would thus dictate against psychological research.

familiar example. We tend to stick to our definitions and under-standings of a concept like education, however, because they are what make most sense to us. Even when people construe things in highly unusual ways (as in delusional thinking), they do so because it makes sense *to them* to do so. Thus, by definition, this tradition in psychology embraces an interactive theory because it assumes that neither a stimulus nor a curriculum can be psycho-logically relevant entities apart from a person's interpretation of them.

With respect to theories of human behavior, the tradition is fairly clear-cut. It refers to those theories that stress individual "construct systems" (perceptions, attitudes, values, understandings) as the fundamental reasons underlying a person's behavior other than his most routine and habitual actions. In brief, a construct system represents a person's knowledge and view of the world. This general theoretical position is represented most clearly in American psychology by such people as Snygg and Combs (1949), Cantril (1950), Allport (1955), Kelly (1955a and b),[6] and Maslow (1962). To a lesser degree, it is reflected in the writings of Rokeach (1970), Harvey, Hunt, and Schroder (1961), and others within the fields of social and cognitive psychology.

Phenomenology in philosophy has historically been one of the perspectives within epistemology concerned with speculation about the nature of knowledge and knowing. Although its roots go back to ancient times, Allport (1955) pinpoints the origins of its influence on modern thought to the views of Leibnitz (i.e., mind is active, purposeful, intentional). He contrasts this view with the logical positivism of John Locke (mind is passive and reactive in nature) and goes on to trace the respective influences of these two traditions—Locke's position prevailing in American and British psychology, and Leibnitz's view prevailing on the European continent. Even today, the bulk of phenomenological argument emanates from Europe.[7] It is interesting to note that the only place where phenomenology, and the existential movement it spawned, has had a reasonably substantial and enduring impact on theory and practice in America is in the field of psychotherapy

---

[6]The writing of Bannister and Fransella (1971) is also relevant, as they have tried to articu-late and champion Kelly's theory in England.

[7]Perhaps the best known Europeans in this country are Polanyi, 1958, 1966; and Merleau-Ponty, 1964.

and clinical psychology.[8] It is also an obvious influence in the emerging, and as yet vaguely defined, field of humanistic psychology.[9]

The point to be made, however, is that basic tenets of this philosophical "active mind" conception of knowledge and knowing are shared in psychology—not only by the neo-phenomenologists mentioned above, but by many developmental theorists as well. To simplify matters, this shared viewpoint posits that knowledge of reality is constructed or invented by each person; that it is not represented in any simple way as an aggregation of learned "facts"; that it is not restricted to the "information input" received by the organism, and that it is continually open to reinterpretation of meaning. As Kelly (1970) has put it:

> This is not to say that one construction is as good as any other, nor is it to deny that at some infinite point in time human vision will behold reality out to the utmost reaches of existence. But it does remind us that all our present perceptions are open to question and reconsideration, and it does broadly suggest that even the most obvious occurrences of everyday life might appear utterly transformed if we were inventive enough to construe them differently. (p.1)

It is in this basic conception of knowledge that a revised methodological paradigm would embrace both philosophical constructs and the developmental theories of Piaget[10] and of psycholinguistics.[11] Although they have different points of departure and different focal concerns, all of these disciplines view knowledge as the product of an active, theory-building, imagining mind.

By its very nature, then, a revised paradigm for research would have to be as much concerned with the quality of experience and the meaning of behavior as with the occurrence of behavior, and it would not assume that similar behavioral expressions by different people necessarily have similar meanings. Thus, it

[8]For example, Snygg and Combs, 1949; Rogers, 1951; Kelly, 1955 a and b; May, Angel, and Ellenberger, 1958.

[9]See Buhler, 1971.

[10]E.g., Piaget and Inhelder, 1969; Piaget, 1973.

[11]E.g., Lenneberg, 1967; Smith, 1971.

would encourage research and evaluation strategies aimed at eliciting meaning and uncovering various qualities of human experience, thought, and production. Such strategies might include, among other things, an in-depth interview of the kind developed for this study, Piaget's "méthode clinique," observation, the documentation of environments, and the analysis of work products and of language samples. These and similar strategies lend themselves to a potential use that is more in the spirit of inquiry than of "criterion testing."

THE IN-DEPTH INTERVIEW AS A RESEARCH METHOD

An in-depth interview with teachers is not a common procedure in educational research. Although we have provided a general rationale for its use, its potential limitations should also be examined and its connection to our theoretical position made clear. The in-depth interview was most widely used as a research method in studies of parental child-rearing practices during the 1930s and '40s. In that context, the validity of the interview was legitimately criticized. It is questionable, at best, to assume that retrospective impressions from parents about their child-rearing practices constitute adequate support for constructing a picture of what really occurred, and it was the specifics of behavior that actually occurred which were of interest to these investigators.

Many questions in our interview dealt with what teachers thought about various issues; others probed for concrete descriptions of the ongoing life of the classroom. Although we have generally taken teachers' descriptions of children's activities and of their own classroom behavior at face value, our major interest has not been in the specifics of the behavior per se. Our concern is with *what the described behaviors represent.* What understandings and perceptions do these behaviors reflect? The strength of an interview lies in its ability to elicit personal opinions, knowledge, understandings, attitudes, and the like, and accumulated evidence of this nature does provide adequate support for reconstructing a general picture of construct systems. Any two teachers will necessarily differ in the specifics of their accounts of a "typical classroom day," but the general understandings they reveal about curriculum and about children in these accounts may be quite similar.

The conceptual framework of this study does not rely heavily on assumptions about the actual occurrences of specific instances

15

of behavior. Rather, it assumes that teachers' characteristic beliefs about children and learning have pervasive effects on their behavior, influencing the learning environment that they create for children and for themselves. Teachers with similar constructs may well foster similar kinds of growth and awareness in children, although they may differ markedly in behavioral specifics. This, at least, is the prediction that derives from a phenomenological theory.

THE THEORY OF PERSONAL CONSTRUCTS

Many psychologists within the neo-phenomenological tradition have created terms to indicate a person's internal perspective, terms such as "life space," "assumptive world," or "belief system." George Kelly's (1955) phrase "personal construct system" seems particularly appropriate, however, because it so clearly suggests an image of man as activist, as constructing something, and this is the image central to all of phenomenology.

We are not drawing on Kelly simply because of his terminology, however. Personal construct theory is one of the most comprehensive theories in psychology. Although Kelly developed it and applied it within the field of psychotherapy, it is applicable to almost any setting. Perhaps the best introductory statement to personal construct theory comes from Bannister and Fransella (1971):

> What a person does, he does to some purpose and he not only behaves, but he intends to indicate something by his behaviour. Indeed, in construct theory terms, behaviour becomes not a reaction but a proposition, not the answer but the question. . . . Behaviour, like words . . . , has *meaning* and changing and elaborating meaning at that. (p. 46)

A personal construct means just what the phrase implies: a personal construction or representation of some aspect of reality that is the result of an individual's interpretation of his world. A construct may be likened in some respects to a concept; it refers to objects or events that a person categorizes in his mind as somehow similar in meaning. It is unlike a concept in that its boundaries—its range of convenience or the range of experience to which it applies—are personally defined on the basis of each individual's past history. Constructs, however, are not merely ways of interpreting and labelling what has happened; they are the means by which we predict and anticipate events, as a

16

forerunner of action. The teacher who construes block building as an exercise for large-muscle development will make different predictions about this activity and undoubtedly act in different ways from one who construes it as "play" or from another who construes it as the child's concrete representation of his thoughts.

To the extent that a person is open to feedback about the consequences of his action, predictions via constructs will sometimes be confirmed and sometimes be found wanting. Thus, the revision of constructs is seen as a function of a person's willingness to act on his own best judgment and his openness to feedback from the environment. Simply "having a new idea or feeling," although important in its own right, is relatively inconsequential for effecting change. Translating an idea into action and experiencing its consequences counts for much more and constitutes the basis of personal (as opposed to "academic") knowledge and learning. This last assumption points up the obvious importance of experience in shaping personal constructs. If significant change is to occur, it requires a quality of experience that supports personal exploration, experimentation, and reflection.

There are other factors inherent in the person that also influence change. One of these is the permeability of constructs. The permeable-impermeable dimension refers to the degree to which a construct can assimilate new elements and thereby generate new implications. Some constructs are, by their very nature, fairly impermeable for most people. We readily apply the construct of "electrons" to electricity and matters of physics, but we rarely find that its meaning can be extended much beyond that. A great many of our constructs about people and life and learning, however, are potentially quite permeable. People who generally deal with life in terms of permeable constructs can use their constructs to make sense out of new situations or new events that confront them. Their thinking is flexible. In contrast, as Bannister and Fransella point out, "if our constructs tend to be impermeable, then we may take pains to make sure that we do not encounter 'new' situations, or else we may force them into the existing system, however bad the fit" (p. 29).

People also apply constructs in ways that can either restrict or enlarge their thinking. Kelly classifies these different uses according to the control the construct exercises over the elements that comprise it. A preemptive construct literally preempts its elements for exclusive membership in that construct only. This is tantamount to saying that if a child is mentally retarded, he is *nothing but* a mental retardate. A person applying such a construct finds it difficult to think about mentally retarded children in any other terms. A stereotypic construct is one that fixes its elements into a predetermined set of other constructs. The mentally retarded child is also construed as an unmotivated child, a physically uncoordinated child, and an often emotionally disturbed child. A propositional construct, on the other hand, places no restrictions on its elements regarding their membership in other constructs. It carries with it the implication that people and events can be construed from many different viewpoints. A mentally retarded child may be a slow child, someone who has just learned to play checkers, and who is handsome, modest, a friend. The more we traffic in propositional constructs, the richer our world becomes, because chances are enhanced for elaborating our understandings and meanings and for rethinking our outlooks. The greater a person's capacity to use constructs propositionally, the more capable he is of modifying and accommodating new information.

Constructs are organized in hierarchical fashion into construct systems, with some constructs being subordinate to others. Depending upon the situation, a person may interpret it and react to it in terms of a lower-order construct. In situations that have importance for a person's image of himself, however, superordinate constructs are applied. Changes in thinking also occur when construct systems become reorganized and constructs take on differing orders of priority.

The central tenets of personal construct theory are stated in the form of a fundamental postulate and eleven elaborative corollaries. For our purposes, this brief discussion of the theory is adequate for acquainting the reader with general concepts found in later chapters. It should be emphasized that we have not set out to "prove" personal construct theory. That is not our goal. We have used the theory because it provides a particularly helpful framework for understanding both the rationale and the results of the interview study.

VALUES, EVALUATION, AND RESEARCH

As noted at the beginning of this chapter, the position we have attempted to argue is based on assumptions and values that are shared across disciplines. That behavioral science operates in an objective (in the sense of value-free) fashion or that evaluation leads to objective (value-free) decisions are myths that have been

18

too long with us and far too widely perpetuated. The latter myth is particularly destructive to the degree that people in education actually believe it, as many apparently do. Decision-making is invariably a subjective, human activity involving value judgments (or weights) placed on whatever evidence is available to the decision-maker. Depending on the extent to which parties to a decision agree that the available evidence has been impartially gathered and represents "important" information, people may or may not agree on the meaning of the evidence. Even when there is virtual consensus on the "facts of the matter," such facts do not automatically lead to decisions regarding future action. People render decisions; information does not. An instructive example of the human reality of decision-making is provided by the biologist René Dubos in describing the diverse reactions of fellow scientists to his book, *Only One Earth: The Care and Maintenance of a Small Planet*:

> Starting from the same set of scientific facts, the experts arrived at a multiplicity of conflicting conclusions with regard to the practical policies concerning the environment—policies, for example, about nuclear energy, pesticides, further industrialization of the world, et cetera. Their conflicts originated not from differences in knowledge or interpretation of facts, but from differences in the value judgments they put on these facts. In this regard, experts display as much diversity as nations and individual persons; they differ not only in their approach to social and human goals but even more, in the selection of these goals. (1972, p. 508)

Although it is understandable that the term "evaluation" might gradually come to be applied to the activity of gathering information and analyzing it prior to decision-making, it is not at all clear why the human activity of actually "evaluating" the information has been so left out of the publicized picture. If the values that dictate educational decisions remain unexplicated— if, by default, they are the implicit values built into the evaluation paradigm itself and the information-gathering instruments it generates—then we are indeed settling for more or less "impersonal decisions," but they are hardly "objective decisions."

In summary, educational decisions are never inherent in research or evaluation studies. They must inevitably be mediated by values. What characterizes rational decision-making is that the values in question be articulated and justified by public criteria rather than by personal and unexamined preference.

19

CHAPTER
2
OPEN EDUCATION AND TEACHER
DEVELOPMENT

The term *open education,* as used in this report, is not intended to refer to an educational program in the usual sense of the word *program.* Rather, it refers to a philosophical and theoretical position: a set of shared ideas about the human capacity to learn, about the nature of human resources for learning, and about the kinds of environment that facilitate and encourage the realization of those learning resources. The position constitutes a framework for the development and evolution of classroom practice, but it does not define or delineate a "model" classroom. Specific assumptions and ideas underlying the theory and practice of open education may be found in several sources. Some of these ideas will be discussed in the context of the chapters that follow, but it is not the purpose of this brief chapter to try to paraphrase succinctly what other people have already stated comprehensively and well (see, for example, Blackie, 1967; Hawkins, 1974; and Weber, 1971). Our only purpose here is to emphasize the teacher's responsibility for decision-making in open education and a conception of ongoing support for teacher development that accompanies this assumption.

It seems important to underscore the teacher's responsibility for decision-making because some market publicity suggests that implementing an open approach is a relatively simple matter of introducing exciting new materials and activities in the classroom, and it depicts the learning that ensues in terms of "fun," "excitement," and "autonomy." As Lillian Katz (1972) has pointed out, and as is evident from the accounts of teachers in this study, such presentations are misleading for several reasons. First, open education is concerned with bringing about a sustained involvement in learning more than with capturing children's attention or exciting them. Second, the open education position assumes that a classroom encompasses the full range of a child's emotional life, from joy and tenderness to anger and rage. Third, children do not always experience "fun" in learning. They, like adults, experience plateaus, self-doubt, and periods of frustration when enthusiasm dissipates. Fourth, children do not learn much of any substantial consequence if their learning is entirely autonomous. Fifth, teaching in an open manner is not easy, and there are no ready "how-to-do-it" prescriptions.

In a previous study of an approach to open education (Bussis and Chittenden, 1970), we undertook an analysis of the Education Development Center's (EDC's) Follow Through program. It became clear in this analysis that the type of classroom EDC staff members were trying to encourage did not fit comfortably at any point along the dimension of "child-centeredness to adult-centeredness," a dimension commonly used in contrasting educational programs for children. Instead, it was better seen as a position that was simultaneously child-centered *and* adult-centered. In order to characterize such an approach, it was necessary to consider both the child's and the teacher's contributions to decisions regarding learning. This two-dimensional scheme, shown in Figure 1, portrays open education as requiring high input from both teacher and child, and indicates in a general sense where other kinds of approaches would be located.

Teachers in the two left-hand quadrants of Figure 1 assume relatively little responsibility for significant curricular and instructional decisions. In conventional programs (lower left-hand quadrant), decisions about the course of children's educational activity are basically made by textbook specifications, by mandated syllabi, or by programmed materials. In the less common "laissez-faire" situation (upper left-hand quadrant), decisions are presumably made by the children themselves.

Teachers in both right-hand quadrants assume much greater responsibility for decision-making. Teachers in the lower right-hand quadrant may be very active in examining curricular materials to decide on their appropriateness, in organizing the curriculum, or in determining student progress to decide on next steps, but these decisions are based on a rather narrow range of information about children. Typically, it is information prejudged to be important, and not information the children

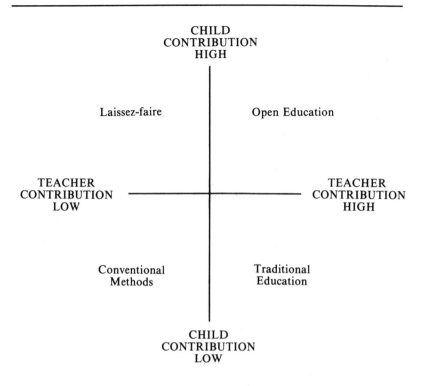

Figure 1. Education Classification Scheme: Based on the extent of active contribution by the individual teacher and the individual child to decisions regarding the content and process of learning.

spontaneously generate in expressing their own learning interests. Decision-making by open education teachers, however, is based on information they gain from the children's own decisions and choices about learning. These are decisions and choices about what to do and how to do it, what purposes to infuse into activities or to impose on materials, and (to some extent) what meanings will be extracted from their varied encounters with subject matter. In order to exercise and develop such capabilities, children must necessarily deal with a curriculum that differs in significant respects from a traditional curriculum. Thus, a primary responsibility of the open classroom teacher is deciding how best to "unpack the curriculum" so that it will be responsive to the interests and needs of individual students.

By "unpacking the curriculum," we refer to what David Hawkins has argued on many occasions (e.g., 1974)—an *accessible* curriculum in terms of the intuitive and associative approaches to knowledge that characterize the native learning style of children. The following excerpt from an informal talk illustrates his concern:

> The subject matter is organized, in the standard curriculum, logically; and I don't want to disparage logical organization. It is simply one kind of organization and not the other kind. By logical, I mean minimally redundant. You start with certain basic propositions and you pursue them through a series of developments, adding information perhaps along the way, but you get the impression, and it is a correct one, that the only way you can get into this is through the first page. From then on it is inaccessible. And that means that the surface area of contact between the subject matter and the learning mind is very very small; there is only one way to get into it. The alternative which you discover as a teacher, of course, when you have to work with diverse human beings in diverse contexts, is that you must yourself reorganize, in your own understanding, your knowledge of that subject matter. And you reorganize it according to a different principle than that of the textbook. . . . By spreading way out, by making many parts of the logically organized subject matter accessible to the already established means of knowing, and interests and commitments of the learner, you greatly . . . increase the probability and the rate of learning in that subject matter. (1973)

Hawkins' analysis centers on the *content* of curriculum, and thus differs from technological approaches to curriculum development which historically have been concerned with the methods and sequence of presenting content.

By divesting subject-matter content of its linear organization and "spreading it out," multiple entry points into knowledge can be created for children. Understandings of balance and symmetry, for example, might be developed from a beginning of block construction, of making mobiles, or of exploration with balance scales. Similarly, contemporary studies in linguistics and reading (e.g., Smith, 1971) indicate that no one entry point into the reading process is suitable for all children, nor is there any invariant set of subskills that characterize the good reader. Important concepts dealing with the animate and social world might be approached through representational play, through the care and observation of animals, through surveys of the school and community. This means that children, like all human beings, learn similar things in quite different ways, just as they derive different understandings from objectively similar experiences. Such a view also suggests that any one activity or encounter (whether with balance beams or puppets) involves many possible concepts, and that any given conceptual problem may be touched on in diverse encounters.

In summary, open education does not argue that subject matter should be devoid of organization—but that schools should provide for diversity in the ways whereby individuals construct coherent systems of thought and meaning about the social and physical world of subject matter. Finally, the open education position would assume that this construction process utilizes all of the human resources for learning and knowing (from sensorimotor, to aesthetic, to emotional) and not just verbal and logical capacities alone.

"Unpacking the curriculum" is a difficult undertaking at best, and it involves a paradoxical twist. The more a teacher progresses toward achieving this goal, the more he creates a new array of decision-making responsibilities. At an obvious level are decisions about providing for learning in the physical arrangement and in the materials of the classroom. At a subtle level are decisions regarding the maintenance of learning when children need help. They may need help in making connections to previous learning, in seeing implications for a future activity, in sorting out critical feedback and extracting meaning from certain situations. Some may need considerable help in getting settled down and involved in the first place. The task of encouraging and guiding children's learning entails key decisions as to whether, when, how, and for what purpose to intervene in a child's activity. These decisions cannot be made by a textbook or teaching manual, although books and manuals may have useful suggestions. Ultimately, they are decisions that can be made only by an adult who assumes responsibility for the learning of individual children. As Hawkins (1974) has stated it:

> The relationship that develops with different children will be different just because they are different children.
> When *you* give a child a range from which to make choices, the choices *he* makes, in turn, give you the basis for deciding what should be done next, what the provisioning should be for him. That is *your* decision, it's dependent

on *your* goals, it's something *you* are responsible for—not in an authoritarian way, but you do have to make a decision and it's your decision, not the child's. If it's a decision to let him alone, you are just as responsible for it as if it's a decision to intervene. (p. 56)

Thus, decisions concerning curriculum and intervention predominate in the instructional life of an open classroom teacher. The fact that these decisions are based on information gained from children's choices is what lends an unusual quality to the upper right-hand quadrant of Figure 1—i.e., where there is high input from both the teacher and the children. Decision-making of this kind on the teacher's part draws on understandings of subject matter and curricular materials as well as on understandings regarding the nature of children's learning; and these are understandings we probed in the interview study to help clarify teaching constructs that are characteristic of that upper right-hand quadrant.

The decision-making demands described thus far may seem unrealistic for anyone other than the most skilled practitioner. This might well be the case if the concern for teacher responsibility in an open approach was not matched by a commensurate view of support for teacher development. Support strategies are an integral part of the open education position. Whatever the specifics of a particular strategy, it emphasizes two essential conditions: a conception of the teacher as a person with potential for professional growth, and an environment that is supportive of the exploration and reflection necessary for change and for continuing development. Within the traditional world of elementary school teaching, however, these conditions have been more conspicuous by their absence than by their presence. The following section discusses assumptions and patterns that have typified the in-service experience of many teachers and examines a more vital approach to teacher development.

IN-SERVICE TEACHER DEVELOPMENT

The first one or two years of teaching experience are generally viewed as the most critical and the most difficult—a period when the basic skills necessary for classroom functioning are presumably developed and mastered. From all accounts, these skills are generally learned behind the classroom door and without much help from colleagues. As Lortie (1969) has summed up the practice of beginning teaching, "Elementary teachers learn their core skills in isolation from other adults" (p. 28).

26

Adult stimulation is, of course, available in graduate work, sometimes undertaken voluntarily by teachers and sometimes mandated by the school district or system. But in either case, graduate courses offer the possibility of only sporadic stimulation and fail to provide sustained support for development. Even worse, according to Sarason (1971), many teachers do not "see the relevance of these courses to their daily work in the classroom" (p. 164), an observation confirmed by our own experience in talking with teachers. With a few notable exceptions, the fare offered by most academic courses (whether sponsored by a graduate institution, a school district, or some other source) is not considered very relevant or nourishing to life in the classroom. At best, courses are seen as intellectually invigorating in an abstract sense.

Aside from formal course work, the years following that critical early period are usually not regarded as years of learning and further conceptual development. Although certain refinements may occur, for all intents and purposes the newcomer has been transformed into a classroom teacher, and that is where matters are left to rest. Sarason (1971) speaks further about in-service development when he notes the consequences of the "routinized existence" of teachers:

> Without exception those who have been teaching for five or more years admitted that they no longer experienced their work with the enthusiasm, excitement, sense of mission, and challenge that they once did. . . . For the most part, they felt as competent as they ever were going to feel, and they verbalized no expectation that they would be teaching or thinking differently sometime in the future. . . . In one way or another these teachers indicated that they rarely experienced anymore the sense of personal and intellectual growth. The shape of the future was quite clear and there were aspects of it that bothered them. The future contained a routine with which they were already quite familiar. (pp. 163-164)

To say that elementary teaching has traditionally been routine and lacking in conceptual challenge is not to say that teachers have always done the same things year in and year out. The recent past has indeed seen new methods, materials, and organizational concepts for the primary grades. In a great many cases, however, these innovations have been conceived, designed, and installed in school systems by people who have regarded the teacher less as a source than as a conveyor of ideas. Consequently, the training efforts undertaken in conjunction with a new method have been

27

geared to shaping the teacher to the method. Rarely have teachers been offered an opportunity to become a contributor, transformer, or critic of the method. Thus, the "innovators" in elementary education of the past few years have tended to retain a traditional view of the teaching role, while attempting to change its specific manifestations. Although significant effort and monies have gone into these projects, the significance of change that has been effected in the majority of American classrooms is questionable (see, for example, Goodlad, Klein, and Associates, 1970; Sarason, 1971; and Smith and Geoffrey, 1971).

Rather than trying to implement a prescribed set of innovative practices, the open education movement has concentrated on a reformulation of traditional ideas about teacher development. Given the teacher's central responsibility for decision-making in an open setting, a more comprehensive view of in-service support seems absolutely necessary. Thus, considerable attention has been given to the problem of creating conditions for continuing growth and self-renewal, both within the schools and without.

One important form of response to this problem has been the emergence of advisory programs, teacher centers, and workshop centers in recent years. (For a review, see Devaney, 1974.) In general, advisory programs are based at a central headquarters, but the advisors work with teachers, children, administrators, and other school and community members *at the school site.* The activities of a workshop or teacher center staff are conducted at a site away from the school, and they usually involve teachers and others from diverse school settings. It is interesting to note that many of these support agencies (including groups that collaborated in the present study) have recently moved in the direction of achieving some blend of the on-site advising strategy together with workshop activities housed at a permanent facility or center. Since all of these agencies offer advising services, we will refer to them under the general rubric of "advisory support" throughout the rest of this chapter.

At the broadest level of generalization, advisory programs are intended to foster an attitude of experimentation and research among teachers and other school personnel and to support this attitude by providing both concrete and conceptual assistance in the process of experimentation. As Armington has noted about the change in English schools, "schools and teachers tend to think of themselves as researchers and experimenters, responding to the endless challenge of doing a better job today than was done yesterday" (1968, p. 4). Just as open education

28

encourages teachers to create an environment that will engage the learning resources and support the learning style of individual children, so advisors attempt to create such an environment for teachers.

Although generalizations are hazardous, there are at least three that characterize the philosophy and functioning of in-service advisory support groups with which we are familiar. These generalizations deal with *specific interactions, personal involvement,* and *self-sustainment.*

It is true that advisory programs are concerned with promoting a broad understanding of teaching that encompasses theory, but the actual exchange between advisor and teacher is more often than not an exchange over very specific things. Theoretical discussions may well ensue from encounters over specifics, but specifics are the concrete starting point. These specific interactions range from demonstrating how to operate machine tools to bringing a new kind of material or a new book to the teacher's attention. Often, the advisor will enter into a project or activity with the teacher and a small group of children. Discussions take place about room arrangement, what might be done with a child who is unable to settle down, ways to extend mathematical concepts with pattern blocks, the pros and cons of a particular book or reading series, how to house a turtle. Whatever the nature of the exchange, it tends to be relevant to a specific teacher, a specific classroom, or a specific group of children. It seems important to emphasize this fact, because the person seeking generalizations often relegates specificity to a minor role—and to do so misses the reality of teaching and advising. Teachers relate to children over real and specific events and materials, and advisors relate to teachers in much the same way.

The second generalization to be made about advisory support concerns personal involvement in learning. Central to open education philosophy is the assumption that understanding rests on a solid experiential component, and advisory programs attempt to foster this component in two basic ways. One way is by centering on materials and activities of the curriculum—the stuff of subject matter. Advisors encourage teachers to begin to explore curricular materials and to "mess about" with them, discovering their properties and limitations first-hand. The ultimate goal is to have teachers encounter subject matter at their own adult level of understanding and skill. Whether in mathematics, science, sculpture, or natural history, advisors try to facilitate teacher exploration. Using a new technique with clay, putting together the bones of a cat skeleton, inventing a dance pattern, designing and building a small rocket—these activities and many more become the joint ventures of teachers and advisors during intensive workshop sessions.

On a more day-to-day basis, advisory programs emphasize the personal learning that comes through experimental teaching. The tasks of "unpacking the curriculum" and extending children's learning through appropriate interventions are a continuing invitation to experiment in the classroom, and advisors lend support to such efforts. This is why and where specificity as well as diversity come into play, for each teacher's endeavors will be different. Experimentation, if taken seriously and if seriously supported, means that classrooms will evolve in different directions. Even the more fully developed open classrooms in a program will differ in significant ways from one another, the differences reflecting the locality, the children, and the teacher. In fact, if classrooms all looked alike—a *goal* of many educational programs—an advisory program, by definition, would have failed. Inherent in this advisory support for classroom experimentation are two related assumptions. First, the school is viewed as a place where adults as well as children learn. Second, the very process of teaching is construed as a process of learning.

The emphasis on personal involvement in learning touches on the third generalization about advisory support programs. They are intended to foster self-sustaining processes, thereby avoiding any permanent dependency on external advisors. Theoretically, at least, advisory programs attempt to accomplish this goal at two levels: the personal and the institutional.

At the personal level, the goal of advisory support for teachers closely parallels the goal of teachers' support for children. It is ultimately intended to foster a sense of awareness—of purpose and reflectivity. This, of course, gets at the heart of the principle of meaningful choice in open education. The mechanism of self-sustaining growth is considered operative when choice is directed by intention, when it is pursued with purpose, and when its consequences are reviewed reflectively. Open education seeks to create an environment for both children and adults that encourages this kind of self-sustaining choice and decision-making process.

Integral to awareness in teaching is a sense of vocational concern. The philosophy underlying advisory support addresses this issue in much the same manner as Thelen (1973) does when he proposes

30

that *authenticity, legitimacy* and *productivity* are the most fundamental concerns for education:

> An activity has authenticity for a participant if he understands it in such terms that he can participate in it intelligently; if he can assimilate the experience it engenders with other past experiences; and if it is meaningful to him. . . .

> An activity is legitimated by reason, as distinguished from capricious-seeming teacher demand, acting-out impulse, mere availability, or impenetrable habit. . . .

> An activity is productive to the extent that it is effective for some purpose. The purpose may be as clear as completing a defined task or as esoteric as arriving at the sense of the meeting. It is awareness of purpose that makes means-ends thinking possible, allows consciousness and self-direction, tests self-concepts against reality, and makes practice add up to capability. (pp. 212-213)

Presented in this context, Thelen's argument may seem tautological to the extent that he defines vocational concern in terms very similar to those with which we (and he) have defined awareness and self-sustained growth. But if one equates the capacity for self-sustained growth with education, then it is a reasonable tautology. It says, in effect, that the educator's concern is with education—both for himself and for those he serves professionally.

The discussion thus far has been directed to self-sustainment at a personal level. But support for the individual teacher must also be viewed in the context of the working environment—the complex network of social influences that constitutes the school-as-an-institution. It is for this reason that advisors often work with such a wide segment of the school community—parents, administrative staff, custodial staff, community volunteers. To bring the many talents and vested interests of an institution into a harmonious and mutually supportive relationship is a task that requires the cooperative effort of all institutional members. Strategies to help foster institutional change and self-renewal differ more markedly among advisory programs than do ideas about working with individual teachers. For some, institutional change in the direction of self-sustaining mutual support has been both the starting point and the goal of work with individual teachers. For others, work with individual teachers has led to a consideration of the complex totality of the school-as-institution. Because of the intricacy of the problem, the conception and pattern of working relationships between an advisory program and the school institution are not only more varied, they are also less fully developed and less discussed in the literature.

Although the investigation of institutional change was not a goal of the interview study, we did attempt to obtain teachers' perceptions of supportive and inhibiting influences in the working environment. More directly, we probed for perceptions of support from advisors for continuing personal growth and in-service development.

CHAPTER
3
DESCRIPTION OF THE STUDY

In order to investigate understandings and perceptions regarding curriculum, children, and the working environment, we interviewed 60 elementary school teachers who were attempting to implement open or more informal approaches to instruction. These in-depth interviews were conducted during the spring of 1972 at four locations: New York City; Scranton, Pennsylvania; Burlington, Vermont; and Boston, Massachusetts.

Forty-six of the teachers were participating in programs that offered the on-site services of advisors. Depending upon the particular program in question, the term *on-site* ranged in meaning from advisors being in a school four days a week to advisors being at some central location within a community for three days a month. Regardless of the frequency of on-site visits, however, all advisors were responsive to individual requests for classroom visits whenever possible and to specific requests for assistance by mail. To be part of an advisory program also meant that the schools in which these teachers worked had given at least a nominal commitment to the concept of open education.

In contrast, the remaining fourteen teachers constitute what we have come to call a "bootstrap" subsample. That is, they were trying to implement open education in their own classrooms, without the help of on-site advisors and with varying degrees of commitment to their efforts on the part of the school administration. In some cases, administrative support was high;

33

in other cases, teachers felt they were working in virtual isolation. The common denominator among these teachers was the fact that they were all seeking some form of assistance by participating in the activities of a workshop center or a teacher center. But just as the frequency of contact with advisors differed markedly for teachers in different advisory programs, so the frequency of attendance at workshop or teacher centers varied widely among bootstrap teachers.

The sample as a whole, therefore, represented a range of experience and contact with different kinds of organizations sponsoring in-service support for open education. We anticipated that the sample would also reflect a wide range of understandings and perceptions concerning the philosophy and practice of open education. This expectation was based primarily on the nature of the educational approach we were studying. As indicated in the preceding chapter, teachers necessarily move toward open classrooms from many different points of view and with different strengths and weaknesses to build on. Although the same could be said of teachers adopting the most mechanized approach to instruction, the lack of prescribed methods in open education tends to accentuate a central feature of all education programs— namely, the particular construct system of an individual teacher.

DESCRIPTION OF ADVISORY PROGRAMS AND WORKSHOP CENTERS

The advisory programs and workshop centers shared basic assumptions about learning and instruction, just as they stood on common educational ground in their orientation toward children and teachers. Their goal was not to interject a brand new program into the ongoing life of a school, but to create conditions that would facilitate the development of teachers' conceptual capacities and response capabilities. Operationally, these groups were alike in that they had received both public and private funding at various stages in their respective histories.

In other respects, the various advisory programs and workshop centers were dissimilar. In origins, composition of staff, and strategy of work, each organization was different. The paragraphs below summarize their history, characteristics, and work patterns at the time of the interview. It should be emphasized, however, that these are static sketches and that all of the programs have continued to evolve since 1972. For a fuller, more adequate description of the groups, their own publications should be consulted. For a more comprehensive treatment of advisory programs and workshop centers in general, we refer the reader to Devaney (1974).

Community Resources Institute (CRI). The Community Resources Institute was established by its codirectors, Ann Cook and Herb Mack, as an organization to assist school personnel, community members, and university faculty members and students in the investigation of educational options. The Institute's home base, a two-story walk-up on Manhattan's upper west side, offered publications and curricular materials for examination and provided facilities for group meetings and some workshop activities. One unusual endeavor of CRI has been the development of children's books (the "Monster Series"), which incorporate questions and ideas that children themselves have generated in discussing the basic story plots with Institute staff.

At the time of the interview, CRI had been concentrating much of its advisory resources in one school. The directors and a resource teacher spent major portions of each week in this school, working with teachers and children and participating in daily classroom activities. In addition, the Institute sponsored workshops after school and in the summer. Although summer workshops were basically theoretical, the after-school workshops dealt with practical questions arising from the teachers' daily experiences. Thus, they tended to revolve around curricular issues, the use of materials, physical arrangement of the classroom, the development of interpersonal skills to handle a particular child's problem, and other matters of immediate concern.

The Institute staff also emphasized the importance of parent and community involvement in the life of the school. Paraprofessionals were drawn from the neighborhood surrounding the school, and parents were encouraged to participate in and contribute to classroom activities.

Education Development Center (EDC). The EDC advisory program was proposed and organized by David Armington in response to the federal government's request for sponsors to participate in the national Follow Through project. Intended to build upon the Head Start program, Follow Through was initiated in the 1968-69 school year as a massive social action program to provide comprehensive services to low-income communities. Program sponsors in Follow Through were responsible mainly for the educational component of the project, which started at the kindergarten level and extended upward one grade level each year. In the spring of 1972 George Hein was director of EDC Follow Through, and the program encompassed a K-3 grade-level range in most schools.

As part of this extensive federal effort, EDC extended its services from a home base in Newton, Massachusetts, to a wide geographical area stretching from Texas to Vermont and including inner-city schools as well as rural ones. This diversity among sites was matched by a diversity among advisors, as EDC staff expertise ranged from experienced teachers to curriculum specialists to poets and dancers.

The strategies required for establishing and maintaining contact with teachers over long distances necessarily differed from those used by advisors in close physical proximity to the schools they served. Summer workshops were held primarily to acquaint new teachers, aides, principals, and parents with the program, and during the school year the schedule of advising varied markedly, depending upon the particular site in question. At the Burlington site, for example, only one school was involved in the Follow Through program, and two advisors visited that school on an average of four consecutive days per month. During these visits, advisors spent time in the classroom, held workshops after school, met with the principal, and engaged in other similar activities. At the Scranton site, on the other hand, several schools scattered over a wide area were participants in Follow Through. As the program gradually expanded over the years, it became physically impossible for advisors to spend time in individual classrooms on any systematic basis. Thus, the typical pattern at the time of the interview was for two or more advisors to make week-long visits every month or six weeks and to hold workshops after school at some central location within the Scranton area. At all sites, however, EDC attempted to develop local advisory capabilities to carry on the advising work.

The particular EDC sites of Burlington and Scranton were chosen for this study for two reasons. They were within reasonable traveling distance, and they offered schools serving low-income populations that were not part of a large city system.

Open Corridor Program. The Open Corridor advisory program operates out of City College of New York, where its founder and director, Lillian Weber, is a professor in the School of Education. From its inception, the program has welcomed school participation contingent upon several conditions. These include the heterogeneous grouping of children, voluntarism of teachers, and administrative arrangements that permit the sharing of corridor space. This last condition, which gives the program its name, underscores the philosophic emphasis on changing working relationships among teachers by attempting to break down the traditional closed-door practices of elementary schools. At the time of the interviews, the various "corridors" consisted of anywhere from three to six classrooms representing consecutive grade levels (e.g., kindergarten, first, second) that opened onto a common hallway. Teachers and children in these classrooms used the corridor space and the materials in it as a common instructional resource. The mutual planning and interaction necessarily involved in such shared use of space and materials was intended to promote a sense of community among teachers that was regarded as essential for self-sustaining teacher development and the long-range growth of the program.

Each corridor had an advisor who was usually in the school two days a week. All of the corridor advisors in the spring of 1972 had classroom teaching experience, many of them having taught in New York City. The most common pattern at that time was for no more than two advisors to be assigned to a particular school, and no more than two schools to be assigned to a particular advisor. In addition to visiting classrooms and meeting with individual teachers, advisors were also active in organizing corridor meetings, setting up after-school workshops, and talking with administrators and parents. Occasionally, a more intensive weekend workshop was held that brought teachers from different schools together. In line with its emphasis on a "community of teachers" and mutual assistance among teachers, the Open Corridor program was beginning (in 1972), and has continued, to seek ways to develop and utilize the advising capabilities of teachers experienced in the program.

Creative Teaching Workshop (CTW). The Creative Teaching Workshop was housed in a loft on the lower east side of Manhattan at the time of the study. This large and undifferentiated space—once an abandoned warehouse—was transformed by Floyd Page and his staff into a multipurpose workshop, with working areas delineated less by the structural boundaries of walls or partitions than by the functional boundaries of tools, materials, and working surfaces that suggest different types of activity.

CTW began as a New York extension of the Early Childhood Education Study (a project of EDC), and both its physical layout and mode of operation in 1972 reflected its connection with curriculum development projects of the 1960s. The basic purpose of CTW was to provide teachers with many opportunities to manipulate, explore, construct, and otherwise directly experience materials and to experiment with processes that have instructional value. This was intended not only to familiarize teachers with a broad use of materials, but, more importantly, to enhance their understanding of the process of learning through reflection on their own involvement in learning.

Teachers usually signed up for a series of weekly or monthly visits to the workshop. After introducing teachers to the workshop and its functions, the staff was available for guidance and help but did not necessarily take a directing hand in defining the teachers' activities or projects. Periodically, special purpose sessions were planned in such areas as tri-wall construction, photography, or mathematical concepts. These special sessions were at times responsive to teacher requests, and at other times decided by staff interests. Although the mode of operation has now changed, CTW staff rarely visited a teacher's school or classroom at the time of the study.

Greater Boston Teachers Center. The Greater Boston Teachers Center was formally initiated under the auspices of the National Association of Independent Schools (NAIS) in December, 1971. One important stimulus for its formation was the popularity of the NAIS intensive workshops that had been held for several successive summers. These workshops, open to teachers from public as well as private schools, were several weeks in duration. For the most part, they were directed by heads of British infant or junior schools.

The Center was set up by its director, Edward Yeomans, as an agency that could sponsor and coordinate a variety of workshop experiences for teachers during the course of the regular school year. A basic activity of the Center was, therefore, one of identifying institutional and individual resources in the greater Boston area that could be used in conducting a series of workshops. These workshop series, held once a week for a period of six to nine weeks, were housed at different sites within the Boston area—schools, established teacher centers, the Children's Museum, and other similar locations. The various workshop series covered a wide range of topics, from environmental studies and upper-grade mathematics to ceramics and dance.

DESCRIPTION OF THE TEACHERS

The teachers in the study were distributed among the five advisory programs and workshop groups as follows:

Program	Number of Teachers
Community Resources Institute	7
EDC Burlington	7
EDC Scranton	11
Open Corridor Program	21
Creative Teaching Workshop	10
Greater Boston Teachers Center	4
	60

We wanted the sample as a whole to consist of teachers working in urban settings, though not exclusively in large inner-city schools. Aside from this, the major requirement of eligibility for the study was that a teacher had completed at least one full school year of participation in an advisory program or with a workshop center. For the two EDC program sites, every teacher who was eligible within this basic guideline was asked to participate in the study. Seven teachers in the CRI advisory program, all from the same school, were eligible for participation. In order to maintain a manageable sample size for the Open Corridor Program, a stratified random sample of 21 teachers was selected from among 50 teachers who met the eligibility requirement. This sample was stratified in terms of grade level and teaching experience, and the 21 teachers were reviewed by Open Corridor advisors to insure that they were representative of the full range of teachers in the program. The bootstrap sample of teachers attending workshops was also chosen with the aid of Center staff to guarantee adequate representation among those who were eligible. At all sites, every teacher who was asked agreed to be interviewed.

As indicated in Table 1, most of the teachers taught at the kindergarten and primary levels. Two pairs of teachers shared classroom space, but the remainder worked within the traditional elementary school setting of the self-contained classroom (not open space). Class sizes ranged from 18 to 38, with an average of 26 pupils. With the occasional exception of art, music, and physical education, the teachers were responsible for instruction in all major curricular areas. Forty-five teachers had the help of an aide or a paraprofessional at least half of the day.

Somewhat more than half of the group (37) had received their preparation for teaching in undergraduate programs, with either

Table 1

Grade Level(s) Taught at the Time of the Interview

Level(s)*	N
K	10
1	19
2	15
3	10
4+	6
	60

*Thirteen teachers taught a combination of two grade levels. These are classified according to the higher of the two levels.

a major or minor in elementary (or early childhood) education. For the most part, these were programs in state-supported colleges. Fifteen teachers had received their basic preparation in a one- or two-year master's-degree program. The remaining eight had come into teaching through a variety of routes, marked by the gradual accumulation of credits for certification from several different kinds of institutions.

As Table 2 indicates, the range in length of teaching experience extended from teachers in their second year at the time of the interview to one teacher in her twenty-ninth year. Because of the sampling requirement of a full year of affiliation with the advisory program or workshop, there were no first-year teachers in the sample. The years of teaching had been continuous for the majority of teachers, although 16 had interrupted their careers for a period of time, usually for the purpose of raising a family.

Table 2

Years of Experience

Years	N
2-3	19
4-6	15
7-10	14
11-29	12
	60

In terms of locality of employment, the group was fairly stable. At the time of the interview, 42 had taught exclusively in their present school district (39 had been within the same school building for periods ranging from three to ten years). Of the 18 who had held positions in other communities or districts, only seven had taught "out of state."

In summary, the data on background and experience do not suggest that the teachers as a group were especially different from other teachers in similar school settings. If they do constitute an atypical sample, they do so to the extent that they voluntarily became involved in programs advocating change. According to their own testimony, however, the group also reflects considerable variation in the matter of initial voluntarism. Some had a fairly clear understanding of what they were volunteering for ("I thought it was a great thing for the school"; "I observed another teacher in the program for a year before joining."), whereas others had happened upon the opportunity or had chosen to participate because there really was no other option ("It was the only kindergarten opening available.").

DATA COLLECTION

Early in the study, meetings were held with advisors and workshop staff to discuss general plans and to begin arrangements for selecting and contacting teachers. Although the specific steps in approaching teachers varied at the different sites, a common overall procedure was followed. Teachers were first informed of the study by advisory and workshop staff who outlined its purposes and the general content of the interview. In New York City, ETS staff also met with small groups of teachers to explain the general nature and purpose of the study. Teachers were told in advance that the interview would be of two to three hours duration and would be tape recorded, with anonymity of responses assured in any subsequent reporting.

An honorarium of $25 was stipulated for each participant. Depending upon local arrangements, that sum was given directly to the teacher or to the school's open education program.

For the most part, interviews were conducted either in office buildings, in hotel rooms, or in some other setting apart from the school in which a teacher worked. Such settings were more conducive to a leisurely, reflective pace because they were free from the intrusions and immediacy of school-related matters.

41

The length of the interviews ranged from 1 hour and 20 minutes to nearly 4 hours. The average length was 2 hours and 20 minutes, with 75 percent of the interviews ranging between 2 and 2¾ hours. The three principal investigators shared the interviewing about equally.

DEVELOPMENT OF THE INTERVIEW

Basic tenets and assumptions underlying the open education position provided a comprehensive framework for constructing the interview. Within that broad framework, however, the interview was further structured by our previous analysis of the dual decision-making process in an open classroom (see Figure 1 in Chapter 2). Thus, one major section of the interview dealt with teachers' understandings related to curriculum and to the utilization of children's resources in learning and instruction. We refer to this as the *curriculum/child* portion of the interview throughout the remainder of the book.

A second factor that shaped the construction of the interview was the concern for teacher development shared by the cooperating open education programs and support groups in the study. The concept of teacher growth and development discussed in Chapter 2 is not wholly innovative. Concrete ideas about how best to actualize teachers' resources for continuing growth, however, have only recently begun to be formulated on the basis of the practical experience of various in-service support agencies. Such groups are a new phenomenon in American education, and they tread on virtually unexplored terrain insofar as research is concerned. Construction of the second part of the interview consequently received little guidance from any theoretical blueprint, but we attempted to focus it on teachers' perceptions of support from advisors and from workshop experiences as well as on their perceptions of other significant influences in the school setting. We refer to this section throughout the book as the *working environment* portion of the interview.

In Chapter 1, the strength of the interview as a research instrument was equated with its ability to elicit personal opinions, knowledge, and understandings—the type of evidence necessary to obtain a general picture of personal constructs and construct systems. We should emphasize here that this is a potential strength of the interview, not an inherent strength. In our experience, at least, the process of developing a final form of the interview for use in the study extended over an eight-month period prior to the beginning of data collection. During that time, several versions of an interview were tried out or piloted with a total of 15 teachers from the local area. Various drafts were also discussed with advisors, with workshop staff, and with other consultants for their comments and suggestions. The process of development, trial, and revision served two major purposes: evaluating the theoretical and practical significance of the content of questions asked, and improving the format or manner in which this content was presented. A copy of the version of the interview used in the study is included in Appendix 1. Even though this represents a "final version" insofar as the present study is concerned, the process of development and revision is a never-ending one. We have continued to revise and adapt the interview for use in other studies.

Although there are no hard and fast rules for developing "productive" interview questions, certain patterns did emerge during the course of the piloting phase that are worth noting. First, questions phrased at a high level of generalization turned out to be answerable only by abstractions and generalities too vague to be revealing of personal constructs. The following is an example of one such question, discarded rather early in the piloting stage:

> On a general level, what do you think is the teacher's responsibility for children's emotional growth?

The purpose behind this question is valid, but it offers no ready entry through personal experience and thus was not conducive to the formulation of personal knowledge and ideas. In fact, it seemed to impede the formulation of coherent personal statements. Where does the teacher begin in responding to such a question—especially if his or her views about emotional growth are complex?

A second unproductive pattern that emerged during the try-out process involved questions dealing with open education per se. Although we attempted to avoid such questions as a rule, we did try a few, and these also tended to elicit slogans and generalities unrevealing of the teacher's own thoughts and perceptions. Thus, only one question in the final version of the interview is addressed (obliquely) to the general topic of open education.

The type of question that more readily brought out personal constructs was one posed with concrete reference to classroom materials, to classroom practices, or to children's behaviors.

> What about natural and environmental materials—sand, water, rocks, plants, tin cans . . . and so on? How valuable do you think this type of material is? Why?

43

How about children who show little apparent interest in anything that you have in the room or who can't settle down and get involved? How do you deal with that situation?

In responding to such questions, teachers could develop and communicate their more abstract and theoretical ideas through specific reference to the ongoing life of the classroom.

Sequencing of the questions was also an important consideration in constructing the interview. The first major question, for example, calls for the description of a "typical day." As an opening, it permits the teacher to start out on familiar ground and enables the interviewer to gain a sense of daily routines and of the teacher's general approach to instruction. This shared background information frequently proved important for understanding and clarifying the discussion of subsequent questions with a more restricted focus. Thus, the type of sequence we found generally most effective (within questions that had many parts as well as within subsections of major portions of the interview) was that of funneling from more open-ended questions to more specific questions.

The interview is only semi-standardized in the usual sense of the word *standardized*. That is, it specifies the overall sequence of questions, the initial wording of questions, and the probes (if any) for each question. Since it is intended to elicit personal constructs, however, a certain amount of informality in its presentation and flexibility in its use is essential.

One important judgment required of the interviewer involves the appropriate use of probes. The following question illustrates a case in point.

With children involved in different activities, on what basis do you divide your time and attention among them?
Probe for:
- is allocation of time and attention a problem for you?
- has it ever been a problem?

Some teachers tended to dwell immediately on the problematic aspects of allocating their time and attention, so much so that the interviewer had to probe for an answer to the original question. Other teachers implied or mentioned in passing the problems of allocating time. In these instances, the interviewer may have chosen to reword the probe slightly to indicate that the problem had been "heard"—e.g., "Can you elaborate a bit more on the problems that seem to arise in dividing your time and attention among the children?" Still other teachers answered the question without a hint of any problem, and the probe was asked as specified.

Another type of judgment necessary for optimal use of the interview is that of ascertaining when to request illustrations if responses seem too abstract, and,conversely, when to press for generalizations if responses seem too enmeshed in detail. Interviewers must also be able to clarify the intent of any question when necessary and to decide whether to discourage or encourage a line of thought that is only tangentially related to a particular question but that appears potentially relevant to other questions.

In order to exercise these kinds of judgments within reasonable bounds, interviewers must agree in their understandings of the purpose of each question. In the final analysis, it is only shared understandings of purpose and intent on the part of the interviewers that serve to "standardize" a procedure intended to uncover personal constructs. Just as a Piagetian interview with children is successful to the extent that the purpose of questioning is honored even though the wording may be varied to suit a particular child, the same is true of any flexible interview. In this study, the fact that the interviewers were the ones who actually developed the interview contributed substantially to the establishment of shared understandings.

CODING SCHEMES AND PROCEDURES

The basic data of the study—the taped interviews—are as phenomenological in nature as we could obtain. Although the interview questions themselves were not ambiguous stimuli, they nevertheless stimulated the expression of very different conceptions among the teachers. The coding schemes impose particular kinds of structure and organization on these otherwise personal and phenomenological data.

All of the coding schemes represent some blend of theoretical rationale and empirical information. That is, they were derived both from the theoretical considerations underlying construction of the interview and from the actual content of teachers' responses to the interview. The schemes vary considerably, however, in the degree to which either theory or empiricism dominates the blend.

Throughout, the more theoretically oriented coding schemes have played the more central role in data interpretation. These schemes are presented in subsequent chapters in which major results of the study are discussed. The following chapter, for instance, describes the coding of teachers' curricular priorities. Because child development theory figured heavily in constructing the curricular priority coding scheme, it contains some highly predictable categories. But even this scheme could not be fully developed without knowing what teachers actually said. Thus, the curricular priority of "children demonstrating basic facts and skills expected of them at a particular grade level" is not a priority grounded in theory. It is a priority grounded in the actuality of teaching and of the pressures that surround a teacher. Although we may have expected such a priority, we had to "hear it" in order to include it in the scheme.

In short, the theoretical categories included in coding schemes represent a rationale we believe is integral to the philosophy of open education. These categories would have appeared in the schemes even if they had failed to describe a single teacher who participated in the study. Indeed such a finding would have extremely important implications, had it occurred. The other categories appearing in theoretically oriented coding schemes reflect themes conveyed by the teachers that differ either mildly or radically (and degrees in between) from the rationale represented by theoretical categories.

Other coding schemes were more empirically derived and serve the express purpose of describing the variation that exists among this particular sample of teachers on certain matters. One such scheme, for example, focuses on the nature and extent of interaction with other teachers in the school. Although we included this coding because professional interaction among teachers is an important concern of open education, the parameters of the coding scheme were necessarily dictated by what the teachers actually said. Still other codings are more accurately described as global ratings. These consist of overall judgments regarding amount of evidence for such variables as anxiety expressed about teaching, and perceived complexity in the roles of other people in the school working environment (e.g., parents, principal).

All coding schemes central to interpretations and speculation we make in this book are presented either in the text or in the appendices. The process of coding entailed listening directly to the tapes. Typed transcripts of the interviews were not used

46

because they fail to capture such rich qualities as the teacher's tone of voice, emphasis, and hesitations—all important data for many of the judgments involved in coding. On the other hand, coders as they listened to the tapes did make written summaries of the content of responses. These summaries, telegraphic in style, retained the teacher's own words and phrasing as much as possible. Since major coding schemes depended on a data base covering long sections of the interview, these notes were important as mnemonic aids to coding decisions. They also helped to offset overinterpretation. That is, coders were required to justify judgments about the underlying meaning of responses by reference to the manifest content of responses.

For the *working environment* section of the interview, which was coded first, formal records of interjudge agreement were made for all coding schemes. Depending upon the type of coding scheme involved, our procedures differed slightly. A sample of five interviews was used to assess agreement on the more complex and the more theoretically based schemes. After satisfactory agreement had been established for the more complex schemes (unsatisfactory schemes were dropped), a separate sample of nine interviews provided the data for testing agreement on the global ratings. We used different interviews for the global ratings in order to reduce any "halo effect" that might have carried over from listening to the original sample of five.

Upon completing development of coding schemes for the *curriculum/child* portion of the interview, we selected 18 teachers who were thought to represent the variation present in the entire sample. Four people, systematically rotating in pairs, coded this portion of the interview. Each coder, paired three times with each of the other coders, listened to 9 tapes. The purpose of this exercise was to establish a concordance in judgment comparable to that of the *working environment* section. At the conclusion of coding the 18 teachers, modifications were made to sharpen the meanings of various schemes and some unworkable schemes were discarded. Half of the remaining 42 teachers were coded by two people working together and making independent judgments, with any discrepancies resolved by mutual agreement or, occasionally, by the judgment of a third person. The other 21 teachers were coded mainly by one person, with a second coder listening only to selected portions of the interview and helping with certain decisions. During the entire course of the project, six coders, including the three principal investigators, were involved at one stage or another.

In discussing the coding process thus far, we have deliberately avoided the technical term *reliability*. To establish the reliability of all coding schemes by traditional correlational procedures would have required an inordinate amount of professional time. As it was, coding entailed at least four hours of work for every hour of taped interview conversation, and the entire process stretched out over a period of two years. More to the point, we did not regard each coding category in every scheme as a separate scale that might be applied independently to data. It would have been virtually impossible to code in this fashion. Our goal was to agree on the variation that existed across scales for each teacher; psychometric standards would have required attention to the variation that existed across teachers for each scale and coding category. Since interpretations of the data rely almost exclusively upon conceptual analyses rather than upon statistical manipulations, we do not view this lack of psychometric reliability as a critical factor. It is simply a factor that should be noted.

In a very real sense, the coding schemes are the most important outcome of the study. They not only define what we looked for and were able to learn from the data, but they have an existence independent of the present data. They constitute a conceptual framework that can serve to orient thinking about teachers' beliefs and pedagogical constructs. This framework is obviously cast in a particular theoretical mold, and where there is an appropriate fit, we hope it will prove useful for furthering theory development as well as for interpreting data obtained from other sources.

CHAPTER
4
TEACHERS' UNDERSTANDINGS OF CURRICULUM

Most people interpret *curriculum* as meaning "a logical organization of subject matter." It seems obvious, however, that neither teachers nor children encounter this conception of curriculum in the classroom. What they do encounter is each other, materials, activities, and a particular physical setting (i.e., an arrangement of equipment and furniture). All of these, plus the school at large and the outside environment, represent potential resources at the teacher's disposal. How and whether a person perceives these as instructional resources, and what learnings they are perceived to promote, determine the nature of an individual's "curriculum construct system." One of the most challenging problems of the study was interpreting the concept of curriculum in a psychological way in order to reflect the broad range of teachers' understandings and meanings.

In attempting to devise a psychological conception, we drew on the linguistic idea of *deep structure* and *surface structure*. In brief, and without claiming to do justice to linguistic theory, the deep structure of a sentence refers to the basic meaning a speaker wishes to express, and is represented by linguists in terms of logical, semantic relationships—e.g., "actor-action-object" for "the dog chased the cat." Surface structure, on the other hand, refers to the perceptible form of a sentence and is represented in terms of conventional grammatical relationships—"subject-verb-object" for "the dog chased the cat." The same basic meaning, of course, could be expressed by a different surface structure such as "the cat was chased by the dog." Precisely how an idea becomes expressed in language is the concern of generative or transformational grammar. Generative grammar refers to the set of rules a speaker unconsciously has at his command for transforming underlying meaning into a comprehensible (i.e., grammatical) sentence. This is a critical concept in linguistics, for if a sentence is ungrammatical[1] it is also unintelligible. The basic meaning of who's doing what to whom, for example, is utterly lost in such a construction as "the chased cat dog the." Thus, the rules of generative grammar are what figuratively "connect" deep structure with a comprehensible surface structure—intention with meaningful expression.

We do not mean to imply any direct analogue between the mental processes involved in speaking a sentence and thinking about curriculum, but the deep structure/surface structure concept is nonetheless suggestive. With reference to the problem at hand, it suggests conceptualizing two levels of a curriculum construct. At one level, curriculum refers to the variety of encounters a teacher plans and provides for children—experiences that are actively encouraged, as well as those that are optional or perhaps merely tolerated. For example, a teacher may plan certain activities that are required of all children—a group meeting at the beginning of the day, reading to an adult, work on mathematics, group singing, clean-up jobs—and at the same time may provide an opportunity for a number of optional experiences—with art, cooking, block building, carpentry, animals, and so on. Because this is what an observer would see going on in the classroom, we have thought of this as the *surface content* (the perceptible form) of curriculum.

At a deeper level, curriculum also has an *organizing content* that consists of the learning priorities and the concerns that a teacher holds for children. To simplify matters, what does the teacher want children to know, do, feel, think, or care about? What qualities of learning does the teacher value and try to promote? In short, what are the teacher's intentions in teaching? If surface content can be considered the *what* of curriculum, then organizing content is the *what for*.

[1]Grammar, in this sense, does not refer to particular forms of expression that are set by the standards of convention as acceptable or polite. A slang expression or a dialectic construction different from standard English can be considered perfectly grammatical. Similarly, the many ellipses that occur in speech do not prevent comprehension because we intuitively understand the underlying grammatical structure of spoken language. If we do not understand the grammatical structure (as when listening to conversation in a foreign language), we may be able to pick out isolated words, but the basic meaning of the speakers remains obscured.

Having distinguished between activities in the classroom (surface content) on the one hand, and learning priorities (organizing content) on the other, a set of questions may be asked about the connections and interconnections between the two. First, what connections does the teacher perceive between his priorities and what is going on in the classroom? For what purposes, in the teacher's mind, are children building a block castle, or pouring water through funnels, or making books filled with their own stories? Second, does the teacher conceive of a particular set of activities as serving only one priority, with a separate set of activities serving another? Or are activities and materials viewed from many perspectives and seen as potentially valuable for a number of learning priorities? The teacher who construes connections between the surface and organizing content of curriculum is better able to transform his intentions for learning into the guidance of learning, and may see new connections in the process. When such connections are noticeably lacking, a child is not likely to receive much guidance or support in the purposeful pursuit of an activity.

THE SURFACE CONTENT OF CURRICULUM

A picture of the surface content of curriculum was reconstructed for each teacher, primarily from responses to questions concerning: (a) the organization of a "typical" day, (b) the kind of planning a teacher did outside of school hours, (c) the physical setup of the classroom, and (d) the materials and equipment in the room (questions 1, 3, 4, and 5 in the interview). Such questions represented a fairly straightforward inquiry into the scope of ongoing activities and the nature of children's encounters. Not surprisingly, the actual range of surface curriculum described by teachers in the study was very broad. At one extreme were those teachers who had departed from their previous conventional curricula only slightly, perhaps introducing a gerbil and some language or math games into the classroom. At the other extreme were those who provided a wide variety of content for children (machines to be taken apart and explored, art techniques such as batik, terrariums containing a number of plant species) and whose "classrooms" literally spilled over into the corridor, the playground, and the surrounding environment. Although all teachers provided for instruction in reading and mathematics, here again there was considerable variation in the range of materials and activities perceived as relevant. For some, basal readers and math workbooks constituted an exclusive focus of interest. For others, such things as dramatic play and cooking were viewed as potentially relevant to the development of language and the understanding of mathematics.

THE ORGANIZING CONTENT OF CURRICULUM

In contrast to our questions about the surface content of curriculum (what was going on in the classroom), we did not ask teachers directly about organizing content—the learning priorities they held for children. Rather, these priorities were inferred from comments made throughout the interview, comments that occasionally assumed a thematic quality in the strength of their conviction or frequency of occurrence. One teacher, for example, continually returned to the theme of wanting children to understand what they do and to develop a sense of purposefulness, a priority that we have labeled "Reflectivity and Intention." This concern first became evident near the beginning of the interview when she was asked about the organization of a "typical" day. She usually opened the morning with a short class meeting to bring certain things to the children's attention or to deal with some matter that needed discussion. By way of illustration, she described that particular day's meeting when they had talked about the rudiments of graphing, "because some of the children were making graphs they really didn't understand." (Her cues to this lack of understanding came from observing the children at work and from some pointed questioning.) In response to questions about the value of semistructured and environmental/natural material, she stressed the importance of material that lent itself to a variety of uses so that children could explore different qualities of a material and turn it to their own inventions and purposes. Still later, in talking about the many benefits of small group work, she concluded with the observation that occasionally a child might get so enthusiastic about "helping" that he would tell another child exactly what to do or give him the right answer to some problem. "I've discussed this with them," she went on, "and tried to get across that I don't care so much if they have the 'right answer,' just so long as they know what they are doing and why." And so it went throughout the entire interview with this teacher, her line of thought returning again and again to the idea of understanding and purpose. Some teachers shared this particular concern; others tended to stress quite different priorities. In all cases, however, there was some noticeable concern or (more frequently) some set

52

of concerns that interlaced the many topics brought up in the interview. These are what were coded as "organizing priorities."

In all, 17 priorities were identified, 11 having a cognitive emphasis and 6 having more of a personal/social emphasis.[2] The most important theoretical characteristic that differentiates these priorities is their comprehensiveness. Some priorities reflected very broad developmental concerns; others, rather narrow and conventional concerns. To illustrate this notion, examples of what were considered "narrow," "middle-range," and "comprehensive" priorities are presented below for both the cognitive and personal/social areas.

Cognitive Priorities

Narrow	*Grade-level Facts and Skills:* Concern that children learn and be able to demonstrate knowledge of the required skills and basic facts expected of them at their particular grade level.
Middle-range	*Initiative/Independence:* Concern that children begin to assume responsibility for their own learning . . . become self-directed in the sense that they need less and less guidance from the teacher.
Comprehensive	*Reflectivity and Intention:* Concern that children know "what they are about and why." Concern that children think through what they are doing, understand (in their own terms) what they are doing . . . interject their own purposes into an activity.

Personal/Social Priorities

Narrow	*Good School Behavior/Docility:* Concern that children conform to a stereotypical pattern of school behavior . . . emphasis on politeness, working hard, settling down, not causing disruptions, etc. This is a concern for socialization into an adult stereotype, with little regard for the nature of children's internal experience.

[2]This splitting of the individual into "cognitive" and "personal/social" components obviously distorts our theoretical position. Nonetheless, it is a cleavage that exists in the language, and we have chosen to stay with the language in the interest of communication.

Middle-range	*Confidence/Contentment:* Concern that children feel good about themselves and their abilities . . . are happy and content in learning, and experience some sense of accomplishment. (This concern lacks the depth and richness of "Awareness and Acceptance of Self," as there is little evidence that the teacher has thought through the meaning of personal growth beyond a "happiness" notion.)
Comprehensive	*Awareness and Acceptance of Self:* Concern that children come to recognize and differentiate their feelings and abilities and accept them as legitimate and worthwhile. Knowing self and experiencing self-respect in order to cope better with life.

All 17 priorities are defined in Appendix 2, but the examples above serve to illustrate that the progression in priorities from narrow to comprehensive involves a shift of focal concern. Narrow priorities, for the most part, are tuned in to a relatively narrow band of behavior that the teacher hopes children will exhibit, the behaviors in themselves constituting major goals of instruction. There is little evidence in the protocols of teachers holding such priorities that they speculate beyond behavioral manifestations to consider the meaning of the behavior for the child. (Almost by definition, "grade-level expectancies" and "good school behavior" are more the concerns of teachers and administrators than of children.)

Middle-range priorities, on the other hand, are characterized by an interest in behavior as it reflects some internal state or quality of the child—in the examples above, confidence and initiative. What makes these priorities "middle-range" in our conception is that the internal states or qualities are apparently regarded by the teacher as basically independent phenomena. For example, a teacher may dwell on such things as involvement, initiative, decision-making capability, and contentment without any suggestion that these are perceived in an integrated fashion. By way of contrast, the teacher expressing comprehensive concerns reveals a higher-order (presumably more synthesized and integrated) concept of internal resources. Thus, ideas of awareness, purpose, understanding, reflection, sensitivity, and reciprocity appear in the thinking of these teachers; they tend to

54

stress the essential integrity of mental life—i.e., the inseparability of cognition from emotion, of intellectual growth from personal growth.

In summary, "comprehensiveness" of priorities refers to the extent to which a teacher evidenced concern for engaging the totality of children's cognitive and/or emotional resources. We would hasten to add that it also refers to the subsuming power of a priority. The teacher concerned about reflectivity and intention, for instance, was not unconcerned about children acquiring facts and skills. On the contrary, these were viewed as important—but important *in the service* of a child's reflective power and developing sense of purpose. They were not viewed as ends in themselves nor as tied to any particular grade level. In general, then, the more comprehensive priorities tended to subsume the less comprehensive.

We say "tended to" in the last sentence advisedly, because the pressure for children to perform at "grade level" or better on achievement tests was felt and discussed by virtually every teacher in the study. The teachers expressing comprehensive cognitive concerns had apparently resolved this pressure (and its attendant anxiety) to the extent that it did not preoccupy them, but it was not at all unusual to hear teachers express middle-range cognitive concerns along with an emphatic, occasionally frantic, stress on facts and skills. In the personal/social realm, it is perhaps obvious that comprehensive priorities did not "subsume" a concern for good school behavior and docility. The comprehensive personal/social priorities were antithetical to such a restricted viewpoint.

HOW CONSTRUCT SYSTEMS DIFFER

Not only did teachers vary considerably in the number and nature of priorities for which they were coded, but also in the degree to which they seemed consciously aware of having priorities at all. There were also vast differences in the number and strength of connections that teachers perceived between their priorities and the surface curriculum. These three components, *organizing priorities, surface curriculum,* and the *connections between them,* comprise the basic ingredients of a curriculum construct system, with various combinations of these ingredients reflecting distinctively different viewpoints about teaching.

What are some of the ways in which curriculum construct systems differ, and how do such differences relate to other perceptions and attitudes? Are different kinds of constructs likely to be associated with different kinds of psychological structure in the classroom? These, of course, are central questions of the study to which we return throughout the remainder of this book, but we will begin to explore them here.

In order to identify different types of constructs, we looked first at the curriculum priorities that tended to dominate a teacher's interview—the one or two concerns expressed most emphatically or frequently. Next, we considered evidence that a teacher was experimenting with the surface curriculum in ways intended to be responsive to the interests of individual children. The four resulting subgroups within the total sample revolved around the "grade-level facts and skills" priority, as follows:

Group 1. (12%) "Grade-level facts and skills" is clearly the dominant priority, and there is little evidence of experimentation or change in the surface curriculum from what the teachers had been practicing previously.

Group 2. (22%) "Grade-level facts and skills" is clearly the dominant priority, but there is much evidence of change and experimentation with the surface curriculum.

Group 3. (39%) "Grade-level facts and skills" is an expressed priority, but not the dominant priority. Middle-range priorities tend to be dominant, and there is evidence of a potentially rich surface curriculum.

Group 4. (27%) A comprehensive or middle-range priority is dominant, and there is little evidence of preoccupation with "grade-level facts and skills" —i.e., it is not codable as such. There is also evidence of a potentially rich surface curriculum.

Strictly speaking, there is no logical reason why a teacher should not have stressed both a comprehensive cognitive priority and "grade-level facts and skills" as dominant curricular themes during the interview. That this did not happen, however, is hardly surprising from a psychological standpoint. To hold the elaboration of intention and meaning together with the demonstration of prescribed behavior as simultaneous "top priorities" would require something close to an extreme form of compartmentalization. Thus, all of the teachers in the study can be described by one of these four very general groupings.

56

GROUP 1 TEACHERS (12%)

Group 1 teachers were doing comparatively little in the way of surface curricular experimentation. For the most part, they planned activities in math and reading that were highly consistent with their dominant concern for grade-level achievement, and they saw the connection between this priority and what went on in the classroom. Thus, the curriculum construct of these teachers tended to be firmly set and relatively impermeable to new elements. One such teacher, in response to a question about the difficulty of building on children's interests, said quite simply, "I don't do that." She went on to say that last year she had brought in a book for a slow reader who was interested in sports, but she had not done much of "that sort of thing this year." Even if these teachers remained conventional in their thinking about curriculum, they did seem to perceive a change with respect to the overall atmosphere of the classroom. Virtually all of them remarked that it was "nicer" or "more relaxed" now, although children generally remained distant in their perception (a characteristic discussed more fully in Chapter 5).

GROUP 2 TEACHERS (22%)

Among the teachers who held "grade-level facts and skills" as a dominant priority (those in Groups 1 and 2), there were major differences in the degree of self-confidence they evidenced during the interview. In fact, Group 1 and Group 2 teachers tended toward opposite ends of the scale on a global rating of self-confidence. By far the greatest uncertainty was expressed by Group 2 teachers who were preoccupied with grade-level achievement but who were *also* experimenting with many surface curriculum changes. Although these teachers introduced new materials and activities into their classrooms, they had difficulty seeing a connection between their innovations and their most deeply held priority. They seemed to believe in an abstract way that worthwhile learning occurred in activities other than math and reading assignments, but they were struggling to understand it and were frequently worried about it. It was as if their relatively narrow priorities did not have the "organizing capacity" to allow them to contend with and make sense of the varied experiences children encountered.

A majority of teachers in the study expressed some degree of uncertainty about one thing or another, but there was a distinctively anxious quality that characterized Group 2 teachers. Had we set out to confirm or "prove" Kelly's theory of personal constructs, we might have hypothesized this finding in advance, for Kelly (1955a) defines anxiety as "the recognition that the events with which one is confronted lie outside the range of convenience of one's construct system" (p. 495). Kelly uses the phrase "range of convenience" here to mean all those things to which a construct comfortably applies—in this case, all those things that the teacher views as legitimate curriculum. This seems a particularly apt description of the teachers we have been talking about. They were confronted with certain surface activities and materials (e.g., block building, a rabbit in the room) that they could not comfortably interpret as curriculum.

It should be pointed out that most Group 2 teachers were experimenting with surface curricular changes because they genuinely seemed to think it was a good idea and that it made teaching more interesting. In contrast, a few teachers were experimenting, to greater or lesser degrees, not so much because they thought it an appropriate activity but because they were in a program that promoted new ways. From the descriptions of their previous teaching experience, which was a recurrent topic with these teachers, we were able to obtain some idea of what their curriculum construct system had been. Perhaps the most descriptive word for this kind of system is "flattened," since the surface curricular activities tend to become organizing priorities in and of themselves. Thus, children work on multiplication problems because they need to know how to do multiplication, or a particular exercise is deemed important because the curriculum guide says it is. The accounts of these teachers were noticeably lacking in depth of rationale for their previous practice, except to refer to manuals and guides, and there was a pathos in remarks that bordered on self-deprecation. One teacher, for example, emphasized that she used to have a curriculum guide and then went on to describe her present situation as "I was just there with my own resources, trying to find the next step and . . . I wasn't sure." Another teacher described the "idea" of the program she was in as "not to use textbooks." She went on: "and it's a problem for me because the District wants textbooks . . . it's very frustrating . . . the program isn't pleased and the District's not pleased with what I'm doing . . . if they could only tell me *what exactly* has to be covered."

As a matter of fact, none of the advisory programs in the study required that a teacher discard any textbook series, guide, or manual, and they all prepared lists of suggested resource material for both teachers and children. Such adjuncts obviously have a place in teaching if they remain subservient to the teacher's own understanding and judgment. However, when they are viewed as replacements for understanding and judgment, the necessary assumption is that teaching is basically a conduit function, with the teacher passing along and "delivering" decisions made elsewhere. Because this assumption is antithetical to what advisors are trying to promote, it is little wonder that some teachers felt at a loss when they could not glean specific and unequivocal directives about what to do in the classroom.

GROUPS 1 AND 2: SECONDARY CURRICULUM PRIORITIES

By definition, "grade-level expectancy" was the dominant priority of all Group 1 and Group 2 teachers. There was, however, a characteristic difference in secondary priorities between the groups. A strong secondary concern of Group 2 teachers, who were experimenting because they thought it a good idea, was the priority of "involvement." In terms of our coding scheme, this meant: "Concern that children become engaged and involved in meaningful activity (as defined mainly from the teacher's perspective) that interests them." Although these teachers genuinely sought to engage children's interests, it seemed as if there was a continuing tension between what was meaningful to the children and what was viewed as academically worthwhile from the teachers' perspective. The meaning of "academic" remained too restricted to accommodate many possibilities other than fairly conventional ones. In one sense, the problem these teachers were experiencing can be construed as a difficulty in elaborating and extending their understanding of worthwhile learning.

Teachers in Group 2 who were experimenting mainly because they were in an innovative program and the Group 1 teachers, who were experimenting only nominally, were characterized by other secondary concerns. They tended to place emphasis on good school behavior, on children being occupied and "busy" during the day, and on rather narrowly conceived socialization concerns. By "narrowly conceived," we mean such things as children learning to share materials, to take turns, to respect the property of others, and so on—with the focus of concern being the manifestation of these behaviors rather than concomitant attitudes and understandings. Thus, the act of sharing was stressed to the neglect of respect for persons. The problem for these teachers (though many of them did not experience it as a problem) was that their priorities and intentions for children contrasted sharply with those held by the advisors.

GROUP 3 TEACHERS (39%) AND GROUP 4 TEACHERS (27%)

Groups 1 and 2 contain teachers who tended to express similar understandings and meanings about the curriculum of open education. A much greater variation was evident among teachers in Groups 3 and 4, both in the nature of the priorities they stressed and in the clarity with which they perceived connections between surface activities and organizing priorities. Before considering the extent of this variation, we wish to comment on a small subset of Group 3 teachers who were characterized by "confidence/contentment" and "grade-level facts and skills" as leading priorities.

The theme of nicer relationships with children was pursued at some length by this small group of teachers. Typically, the surface curricular changes that they described, which were not drastic but represented a substantial departure from their previous teaching and from that of their colleagues, were justified on grounds of the greater confidence and contentment of the children. They saw classrooms as more "natural" and "sociable" environments than before. One teacher, with more than 15 years of experience, noted it was "perfectly natural for little children to want to put their arms around you . . . and we allow them to do it now." She contrasted this with the admonition she had always received in the past: "It's *bad* to get emotionally involved with children." Another teacher lamented the fact that visitors to the school often assumed her class was a "mentally retarded group," simply because the children had freedom to walk around and talk with each other. The meaning of "open education" for this small subset of teachers had little to do with subject matter content; it was almost entirely equated with humanizing the classroom. Although many teachers stressed the importance of a healthy and personally dignifying environment for children, these particular teachers seemed struck by the realization that it was both possible and legitimate to create such an environment in school.

As defined earlier, Group 3 teachers expressed "grade-level facts and skills" as a priority but not as a dominating priority. Group 4 teachers were not coded for "grade-level facts and skills," this priority presumably having been subsumed by the more comprehensive concerns they expressed. Almost all of the teachers in Group 3 and Group 4 described a surface curriculum

60

that provided children many opportunities to come in contact with rich and interesting content. Our interest is in what differentiated the thinking of the teachers in Groups 3 and 4, and with what possible consequences.

CONNECTIONS BETWEEN SURFACE CURRICULUM AND ORGANIZING PRIORITIES: GROUPS 3 AND 4

Perhaps the most provocative finding in our study of curriculum construct systems was the variation among Group 3 and Group 4 teachers in the clarity of perceived connections between surface curriculum and organizing priorities. This clarity was not just a matter of articulation in the sense of well-formulated expression, although articulation undoubtedly influenced our judgments at some level. A much more prominent factor, however, was the teacher's ability to move back and forth between classroom activities and organizing priorities, using a specific encounter to illustrate a broader concern and relating broader priorities back to specific instances. The following vignettes are intended to illustrate "strong" connections as evidenced by an easy transition from surface curriculum to organizing priorities.

Vignette 1. Mack is a first-grade teacher. He works closely with the second-grade teacher, Art, who occupies an adjoining room connected by a passageway. They plan classroom provisions together and exchange children freely, so that everyone in each room has access to all of the materials, equipment, and animals. At the time of the interview, Mack had a paraprofessional working with him and had just been assigned a student teacher.

Mack's two most predominant concerns throughout the interview were *Reflectivity and Intention* and *Awareness and Acceptance of Self.* A hint of these priorities, and what he does to foster them, was evident even in the beginning portion of the interview when the interviewer was asking for routine, background information. He responded with some rather cynical remarks to the question: "How many children are in your class?"

"Thirty. The enrollment was for thirty-two, but one kid never showed. It's great how they got rid of him. They transferred him to 'Not Found!' I got a little slip saying, 'T-Y-R-O-N-E Smith: transferred from first grade—to 'Not Found.' As simple as that. And then another child came in one day and told me he was going to move, and I said 'where?' and he said he didn't know but tonight he was gonna move. He never came back . . . so I guess he did. So now I just have thirty kids."

"How about other children? Do you ever work with any other kids aside from your own and Art's?"

"Well, some fifth-grade kids used to come around after school when Art and I were making stuff. They got interested in the snakes and started to build nice snake cages; and now they come downstairs to my room sometimes during the day. Then three other fifth-graders wanted to come down. I asked them to think about what they wanted to do in the room—either with my kids or without them—and give it to me several days beforehand in writing. Not as an assignment or anything, but so they'd know what they wanted to do; and I could think about it and speak to them before they came down. Just so we could be somewhat organized."

> In the excerpt about the fifth-grade children, Mack made a rather clear connection between his own behavior (requesting them to think ahead and plan what they want to do) and a concern that children act purposefully. Moving on to the first question that constitutes the real substance of the interview, Mack was asked to recount the activities of a "typical" school day, starting with when the children arrive in the morning.

"They come in and I've got a pegboard with hooks and everybody's name on a tag. Under some of the names are numbers that refer to sentences out in the corridor. The sentences describe jobs they have to do on a rotating basis. They're all written sort of the same, like 'please clean the rabbit's home,' 'please clean the crow's home,' or 'please give the crow food,' 'please give the turtles food.' They're all color-coded so they're easy to read; and there's always another adult or child in the hall to help anyone who can't read them. So some kids do jobs right off, and other kids I just help get started. I've asked all the adults to do that. The kids come in at 8:50, and at least 'til 9:15 we just get them settled down and into something. A few children find it very difficult to make a decision, and we clipboard those kids."

"What do you mean, 'clipboard' them?"

"Well, we have clipboards with mimeographed sheets that show every area in my room, and Art's, and in the corridor. What we do is number the areas where we want kids to go, and write in a few directions, so any adult can just look at the thing and see what the

62

child's supposed to be doing. It's interesting—some children view them as punishment (nothing heavy, but still a kind of punishment), and others like it. Some kids who can make decisions perfectly well even want to make their own clipboard assignments, which is fine, too. And I'll occasionally clipboard a kid I saw doing something very interesting during the day, because I don't want him to forget it."

> Opinions may differ about the appropriateness of the clipboard strategy, but Mack obviously viewed it as a safety device against some children wandering around aimlessly—a strategy for avoiding purposelessness. Occasionally, he used it as a technique to reinforce a child's awareness. The important point is that he again made a connection between his own actions and what he wanted to foster in children.

> The implications of the sentences in the corridor describing various job responsibilities were also interesting. Although virtually every teacher we interviewed described clean-up and maintenance activities that children had to do, these responsibilities were communicated orally in most instances. Elsewhere in the interview, Mack stated that he was "superinvolved with reading for a long time, because of the pressure." He went on to say that he now disagrees with this emphasis and doesn't read with the children all the time. What Mack did do, however, was to provide opportunities for children to read in the context of carrying out activities other than "reading" with a capital *R*. We will have more to say about this later.

> The interview continued with a comment about "clipboarding" from the interviewer.

"That's interesting, and you've anticipated some questions I want to ask later about how to help kids who have a hard time with choice. But I interrupted you. Let's get back to the day."

"About 11:30 everybody gets together, and I either read or we have a discussion. The validity of getting the group together is up for grabs, I guess; but I think it's important for everyone to listen at the same time, and to listen to each other, every now and then. It happens once or twice a day that we do this. At the beginning of the year, of course, I had short meetings first thing in the morning to acquaint the children with the room; but we can do away with that now. What I've tried to do in discussion . . . well, I started to

63

ask people what they did in the morning. I wanted them to be aware of what they're doing, 'cause many kids will just remember the last thing they did and whether they hated it or liked it. Now I'm to the point of just trying to get the most interesting thing they did, or the thing they like the most. Not a formal thing like 'Show and Tell' and not everybody talks at every meeting. But I'm just trying to pull something out of the discussion that's relevant to them—to their interests and abilities. I want them to know that."

In describing the activities of the day (the surface curriculum), Mack once more revealed his underlying concerns for *Self-Awareness* and *Reflection;* and he again made the connection between surface activities and organizing concerns an explicit one. The beginning-of-the-year meetings to acquaint children with the room may also be interpreted as an action intended to foster purposeful behavior. Why Mack thought the validity of getting the whole group together may be "up for grabs" is an interesting question. We suspect it is because an open approach is so frequently treated in the literature as a "totally individualized approach," with the strong implication that it is a very particular *method*—a prescribed "it" that does not sanction whole-group activity. This "method-oriented" interpretation is reminiscent of the teacher who described the "idea" of open education as "not to use textbooks." Mack's own rationale for getting the whole group together introduced the first suggestion of a possible concern for *Social Problem-solving and Appreciation of Others*—a priority that became much more evident in later portions of the interview.

So far, the things that Mack's children are doing and "getting into" remain unknown from the interview. A partial list of the surface curriculum he later described includes a large block area; a loft where children read or plan, with a car seat underneath that constitutes a "getaway" place; a large terrarium; a water table; a math area; and a language arts area with a rug, a rocker, and two homemade tables. Extra things in Art's room include wet and dry sand, an art area, and a "gigantic" gerbil cage. There is a piano, a workbench, a dress-up corner, a "store," and drums and other musical instruments out in the corridor. (It was not exactly clear where the crow and rabbit lived, although it was clear they had the free run of all areas on occasion.)

64

Mack described the afternoon activities as starting off with "a sing" in the corridor with the second grade. The prekindergarten and kindergarten classes are usually invited to this event. The children then go back to work in their various activities. Mack continues . . .

"At two o'clock we usually write. Since Christmas, some kids have started writing about what they did during the day or some incident that's happened. Other kids may write about a word like *angry,* or part of a sentence like '*I felt so low, I* . . .' Usually it's an emotional word (an 'organic word,' as Sylvia Ashton Warner calls it). Some kids who can't write so well just have to supply the last word to a sentence like '*Today* I worked . . .' But they have to write out the whole sentence, so it's like a penmanship thing, which I'm not above 'cause you gotta learn how to write sometime. And, again, it helps make them aware of what they're doing in the room. Mainly I'm just trying to show them the whole language bit is a circular thing. Whatever you say can be written down . . . and somebody can read it . . . and you can hear it again . . . and someone else can write it . . . and it's circular. At first, I used to read everybody's writing, and now they read their own and each other's. While they're writing . . . well, everyone's got what I call 'dictionaries,' but they're really Level 1 Spellers that I found down in the basement of the school. They're perfect dictionaries with just enough words in them; and you can always add more 'cause there's lots of space on the pages. Reading's usually going on throughout the day. I've assigned ten children that each adult [Mack, the paraprofessional, and the student teacher] should read with twice a week, plus I also read with some other kids who are having the most problems. Then at the end of the day there are jobs again. Kids who don't have an assigned job can help anywhere they like, but everyone has to help."

To use his own phrase, Mack did not appear "superinvolved" with reading as an isolated skill, but he certainly seemed concerned with putting reading and writing in the context of intentional communication. He communicated meaningful things to the children in writing (as illustrated by the "job sentences" in the corridor); and they, in turn, communicated how they feel or what they have experienced by writing to him and to each other. He also provided each child with an important resource—a dictionary—to help carry out communicative intentions. It is interesting to note that Mack made the distinction in his own mind between children who

65

really want to communicate in writing and those who are contending more with the act of writing itself—those for whom it is an exercise in penmanship.

Mack's organizing curriculum priorities are perhaps best summarized in a later portion of the interview dealing with children's needs and feelings: "I want them to have a sense of self—to know that their ideas and feelings are okay, and that they have knowledge and their knowledge will grow. If they really know that, I don't give a damn what kind of education they run across later in life. I think they'll make it."

This vignette is interspersed with some lengthy interpretive comments in order to illustrate what we mean by "seeing connections." One is not left guessing how this teacher attempts to realize his concerns for children in the ongoing life of the classroom. Connections between surface curriculum and organizing priorities were made clear in response to the very first questions of the interview, and Mack continued to make them clear throughout.

Vignette 2. Jessie is a fourth-grade teacher. She is a middle-aged woman who had previously been in business and had taught for only two years at the time of the interview. The results of her coded interview yielded a profile of curricular priorities similar to Mack's—with strong emphases on *Awareness and Acceptance of Self, Reflectivity and Intention, Social Problem-solving and Appreciation of Others, Reciprocity in Learning,* and a priority labeled *Construct/Discover/Pursue Interest.* This last priority refers to a concern that children sustain an involvement in meaningful activity, as defined from the child's perspective, that leads to new knowledge and insights. We pick up her comments at a place where the interview begins to focus more sharply on children. She is responding to the question: "You've described how the children in your class often work in small groups; what benefits do you see in such groupings?"

"Well, the primary benefit is that children can work in areas that interest them. I don't doubt for one moment that they learn more when they're motivated—because they're learning for themselves and not for me. The second thing is they talk to each other a lot. When they do that, they're defining and redefining their own thoughts as well as what other people say; and that tends to make them more articulate. The other thing I see is that they learn from each other. You know, you couldn't run a class without that. They really *are* the teachers many times."

"Yes, I think I do understand. . . . And you've really already answered this next question about needs and feelings—you obviously think the children express their needs and feelings freely. But does this free expression ever cause any difficulties for you, the teacher?"

"Sure. At the beginning of the year I had a few children who were incredibly angry. I had one boy I only saw in two moods—anger and rage. I used to come home feeling beaten up. It obviously becomes less and less a problem as the year goes on, but you do feel it. But if you say that our affective life is part of our common humanity, then you all feel the effects of life. It's not something where a kid sits at his desk with his mouth shut—whether he's happy, or angry, or whatever. If we can't help a child with an emotional problem, he's not going to learn much; and we're all (the children and I) responsible to some extent. That's what makes it the most emotionally draining job you can imagine."

"What about the children? Does this freedom to express needs and feelings ever cause any difficulties for them?"

"Yes, 'cause we're all in it together. If you're going to relate to each other, you don't relate in a vacuum—you relate around something. And if you relate around something, you're going to have some arguments and difficulties. They get to know each other's little quirks and what provokes people, and occasionally they do provoke each other. But basically it's very rewarding. It's to the point now where there aren't many fights, and the children try to arbitrate any fights that do occur. Just a couple of weeks ago, two boys got into a real bout; and the kids had a 'trial.' I was elected judge, and the whole class was the jury—and it all came off rather nicely. The kids really do try hard to maintain what we have going."

"I was just going to ask what benefits you saw in children expressing themselves freely. Maybe you'd like to comment some more on that. . . ."

"We live together, that's what. We like each other; and we care about each other. Can you imagine sharing a living room with people with whom you only interacted on 'polite' and 'civil' terms?"

> In her initial remarks about the benefits of small groupings, Jessie made some specific connections between her concerns for children and what she encouraged in the classroom. For the most part, however, these excerpts served to reveal her priorities; and they set the stage

by describing the emotional tone of the classroom. The following excerpts make her own role in establishing this atmosphere and in accomplishing her priorities much clearer.

"What about sensitive content—things like sex, death, birth, fears that children have. Do you think such content has any place in the classroom? And how do you handle it?

"I can give you a very specific example. I have this girl who used to write 'pussy' over everything. One day I said to her, 'You know, Janet, the word you're looking for is vagina—that's really what you're talking about.' And she looked at me and kinda nodded her head and said 'Yes, you're right." I had to assure this child, and a few other children, that all girls really have vaginas and all boys have penises. They had wanted to make sure and had been peeking in the bathrooms. They were really worried about it. Kids of this age are absorbed with sex, but they're also embarrassed. One of the other teachers on the corridor brought in a fetus in a bottle, and this led to a whole thing about how a baby is born. I wanted to discuss it with them, because you just don't know what's going on in their heads. They all had ideas, but at first it was an 'unmentionable' subject—they just shook their heads and giggled. So I stopped trying to discuss it; and the next day I got a simplified book on sex that I put out for them to read. Boy, that book just flew around the classroom! And then I found a marvelous picture of a child being born—with umbilical cord intact, and all. I felt the picture could stimulate questions. I knew the kids wanted to know more, but they weren't sure what questions to ask. So I took the picture to the principal and said I'd probably get a lot of flack from parents (which never happened), but would he okay it. He did; and the children looked at that picture for days. And it did prompt all kinds of questions and discussion, like what the umbilical cord is for, and what would happen if you didn't cut it, and where was the best place for the doctor to cut it, and so on. Then another teacher's rabbit had babies; and our mouse had babies, and . . . well, the whole topic of sex and birth is out in the open now and they're not embarrassed any more. They know for sure; and that makes all the difference. So, yes, sensitive content comes up and you have to deal with it. We're into some discussions of drugs now. The kids have seen a lot of it, too much of it, and I think they have to be able to talk about it. If you turn them off—like saying, 'Well, I'll have to think about that for a while'—because you're not willing to face up to it, then it's no good."

"Again, you've already anticipated my next questions about interests. You hear so much in open education about 'building on children's interests,' but how does it really work out in practice? You've just given one very good example, but perhaps you could talk about some other concrete examples of building on interest. . . ."

"Yes, it's their interests—what's inside them—that led to this whole biological, birth thing. But I can give you a simpler example. There were three boys interested in baseball, and they wanted to do a 'win/lose' graph of all the teams. So we talked about it a bit, and they did it, and it was great. Then we got into the notion of comparisons more deeply, and these boys are now interested in all kinds of comparisons. They've compared everything! Lately it's been weight comparisons, and they've set this problem for themselves: 'Do people who are born heavy remain heavier throughout life?' It's an interesting question, and they're trying to figure out how to get necessary data, like birth records, and . . . well, I guess that relates back to the birth thing, too."

> Though Jessie had more to say about building on children's interests, the point is that she, like Mack, could make "connections" between her surface curriculum and her priorities for children.

Although we have tried to maintain the conversational flow of the interview and stay as close as possible to the teachers' exact words in these vignettes, they are, of necessity, edited versions of what was said. Even in edited form, however, the excerpts are not necessarily impressive as models of eloquent speech. What *is* impressive about them is the ability of these teachers to go from organizing priorities to surface curriculum and back again— occasionally in the same breath.

Other teachers, who were reasonably articulate in indicating priorities for children, were more vague in describing concrete connections between these priorities and classroom activities. Some, for example, described the organization of the day without providing much of a rationale for their activities, even when probed by the interviewer. The following are typical examples of varying degrees of "haziness" in making, or alluding to, connections. They are abbreviated responses to the question: "What benefits do you see in small groupings?"

> "Lack of boredom."
>
> "Just as much learning goes on when children learn from each other."

"Freer exchange of ideas; get to know them better."

"Children help and teach each other things I sometimes don't realize they need help with."

"Sometimes there are squabbles and you want them to work it out, because working it out results in social growth."

In general, Group 4 teachers tended to articulate more connections and clearer connections than Group 3 teachers, although there was considerable variation within each group. As indicated previously, however, almost all of the teachers in Groups 3 and 4 described a surface curriculum that provided children with opportunities to come in contact with rich and interesting content, and they all encouraged small group interaction. What, then, differentiates teachers who readily "see" how potential opportunities for valued learning are realized in the classroom from those who do not clearly perceive connections between their surface curriculum and organizing priorities?

One answer to this question undoubtedly resides in a teacher's understanding of children and of child development, the subject of the next chapter. A second answer, however, is suggested by our findings related to materials.

SEEING CONNECTIONS AND THE PERCEIVED VALUE OF MATERIALS

Two questions in the interview (questions 6 and 7) probed specifically for values that teachers perceived in various kinds of material. One focused on the value of semistructured material (e.g., Cuisenaire rods, unifix cubes, balance scales, puzzles); the other focused on the value of natural and environmental material (e.g., sand, water, rocks, plastic bottles, plants, and animals). Unlike the analysis of organizing priorities in which a teacher's responses throughout the entire interview were used as the basis for coding, the coding of "perceived value of materials" was based entirely upon responses to these two questions. The coding categories developed for this analysis are presented in Table 3.

Occasionally, a teacher might make a statement in later portions of the interview that clearly indicated a perceived value of materials that had not been previously mentioned. In such cases, we made an adjustment in the materials' coding, but this was a rare occurrence. For the most part, later comments served to reinforce and provide additional illustrations of perceived values

Table 3

Coding Categories: Perceptions of Materials and Provisions

1. *Valuable for construing many possibilities.* With younger children, the value may be seen in the development of symbolic functioning—i.e., the child can "sever" the meaning from an object and impose his own meaning onto it, using it in a variety of ways. *Or,* the material may lend itself to many possibilities for in-depth inquiry and the pursuit of substantive questions.

2. *Valuable for the richness of experiential learning.* The emphasis here is on the child's direct experience with the material or phenomenon—e.g., experience with sand, water, and blocks promotes ideas of measurement, quantity, space. *Or,* children learn about a particular phenomenon from direct contact with it—e.g., learn about frogs, magnets, machines.

3. *Valuable for teaching a general concept.* E.g., Cuisenaire rods or pattern blocks assist the child in understanding the general notion of fractions. This category of response is occasionally accompanied by comments on the importance of visual imagery or concrete images.

4. *Valuable for personal/social reasons.* The material may be valuable for intrinsic reasons—what it means to the owner or user promotes a sense of integrity or accomplishment— e.g., what a child brings from home is important because it represents his legitimate contribution to the classroom. *Or,* the material may promote valuable social interaction—e.g., children become engaged in discussion around the water table.

5. *Valuable for doing different things.* The emphasis here may be on adding variety to the classroom, or on the fact that children can be "creative" with the material in a variety of ways. The possibilities remain unspecified, however.

6. *Valuable for teaching a very specific outcome.* E.g., children learn that a square has four sides from pattern blocks; or that "four plus one equals five" from a balance beam. The teacher may comment on children "seeing it" for themselves, but there is no mention of imagery.

71

7. *Valuable for reinforcing effect.* A demonstration with materials reinforces or "clinches" a concept taught verbally by the teacher or learned from a workbook.

8. *Valuable for motivational and managerial reasons.* Children may play with materials when their work is done. *Or,* materials are viewed as something to keep children occupied while the teacher works with small groups on an assignment.

---

mentioned in direct response to the questions about materials. It should be noted that the distinction between Categories 1 and 2 became blurred with some teachers, and our coding was based more on a judgment of emphasis: Was the major thrust of the teacher's remarks closer to "construing possibilities" or to "experiential learning"? Some of the categories were eligible to be coded twice. Categories 1, 2, 4,and 8 contain two distinct alternative definitions, and if both definitions were clearly mentioned, each one was checked.

The fact that Category 1 and 2 definitions occasionally blended in the response of some teachers did not pose a serious obstacle for interpretation, because it was *both* categories that characterized teachers who perceived strong connections between their surface curriculum and their priorities. This was not simply a "trend" in the data; it was a striking result, as can be seen in Table 4. Slightly over 50 percent of all Group 4 responses to the materials questions fell in these two categories, compared with less than 15 percent of the Group 3 responses. Equally important, *within each group* it was the emphasis on "construing possibilities" or "experiential learning" that distinguished teachers who saw connections clearly from those who perceived them less clearly.

Although we had not anticipated the magnitude of this relationship between "seeing connections" and differentially valuing materials, it is a perfectly logical relationship in theory. If one considers what gives rise to connections in a teacher's mind, feedback from the environment stands out as one obviously important factor. A person does something, or sets something into motion, or makes it possible for something to happen, and then observes the consequences. To the extent that he is open to feedback about the consequences of his action, his understanding may be strengthened or changed. This assumption, of course, lies at the heart of personal construct theory and the theory of construct change. But openness to feedback, in and of itself, does not constitute a sufficient condition for strengthened or changed

Table 4

Materials Coding:

Percentage of Teachers' Remarks Within Each Value Category for Different Priority Groups

Perceived Value of Materials Coding Categories	Teacher Groups Based on Dominant Priorities			
	Group 1 (N=7)	Group 2 (N=13)	Group 3 (N=24)	Group 4 (N=16)
1. Construing possibilities	—	1	6	22
2. Experiential learning	4	9	7	32
3. Teaching general concepts	14	14	33	15
4. Personal/social reasons	9	1	4	12
5. Doing different things	14	27	28	14
6. Teaching specific outcomes	50	30	14	3
7. Reinforcing effect	4	—	4	2
8. Motivational/managerial value	4	18	4	—
Total %	99	100	100	100

understanding. The feedback obtained from observing must also supply the observer with relevant information—*informational support* that will tend to confirm or deny the effectiveness and appropriateness of his actions. This is where a knowledge of materials becomes critical, because the amount of informational support inherent in the feedback that teachers receive is partially a function of their knowledge about the value of various materials. If a teacher does not see where a child can go with a particular material—if his understanding of the learning possibilities in a situation is limited—then it is not surprising that connections between surface curriculum and curricular priorities are not clearly perceived.

Another way to formulate this interpretation, without giving undue emphasis to the importance of materials, is to think of a given priority as having a valuing component and a cognitive component. It is easy to conceive of the valuing component; the teacher holds the priority in the first place because it is valued. The cognitive component is more complex. Theoretically, at least, the latter consists of all the relevant knowledge a teacher has at his command for bringing about and for recognizing the realization of a priority—including knowledge of materials, subject matter, children, and the learning process. If the cognitive component is relatively weak in terms of a teacher's personal knowledge, then he may provide the classroom with rich materials *on the faith* that they will promote certain learning priorities. Although perfectly appropriate in some situations, action based on valuing and faith may or may not lead to significant learning by children in the classroom situation. More to the point, action based on valuing and faith is not very likely to lead to an enlargement or strengthening of the teacher's own understanding. The potential informational support available in feedback to the teacher is not received because it is not recognized.

Before further discussion of this interpretation, or of other results related to materials, another short vignette illustrates the kinds of things teachers said that were coded in the "construing possibilities" and "experiential learning" categories.

Vignette 3. Stephanie is a first-grade teacher. We begin with her comments on one-inch cubes, a material she had mentioned before, which the interviewer used as lead-in to the question about the value of semistructured material.

"Cubes can be used to begin children on area. One child, for example, marked off a large square in our room to find out how many of these cubes covered it . . . and she counted them. They're useful for children who can't do addition yet in their heads and who don't count on their fingers. The unifix cubes can be used for all kinds of measurement—a person's height, the length of a table . . . if you have enough of them, you can measure the length and width of the room. It really can move into so many directions. Like the children use them to make planes . . . "

"Planes?"

"Planes, right. They'll use them when they build things. Or we had a race with cars and the children used them to find out—to count—the differences between the distances the cars went. Or you can use them for money. One of my boys used them for poker chips when he was teaching some other boys how to play poker. Even for art collages . . . you can use them for that."

"Are there any limitations or drawbacks to these materials?"

"Well, I've bought most of my materials and I've been careful about the things I've bought. I usually buy something that has many purposes ... that you can use for many things. I went over the catalog several times before deciding, so I haven't really been sorry about anything I've bought this year. Like the Lego set we got. You might think the children would just build cars and things like that, but they're really getting a feeling of how gears work and how machines work. They've *seen* gears when they've taken apart the machines I was telling you about, but those gears are sharp and you can't work with them very well. But these they can work with. One boy put together a structure so that when one gear turned, another one turned, and that made another one turn. So he's really gotten onto a feeling of machinery."

"How about natural and environmental stuff—like sand, water, plants, plastic bottles—how important are they? What value do you see in that kind of material?"

"I think all of those things are important. Having a water table, or a place to put water, is really great."

"Why is that?"

"First of all, children like working with water because it's a very soothing experience. Like sometimes if a child is upset and just goes over and works with the water, it has a very calming effect on him. And he usually gets very involved. And . . ."

"What is he doing when he gets involved?"

"He's beginning to understand that water takes the shape of the container. Then he might begin to understand that some things float and some things don't float, and there must be a reason— like he might get into boats then. Then he might get into math because he has small containers and large containers, and he's filling up the large ones with the small ones to find out how many small make one large. And then they have hoses, of course, and they find out how to get water from one bottle to another without actually pouring it—the siphoning idea. Or they'll experiment with blowing in, and creating a vacuum. They've done a lot of experiments. Some of the children made a witch's potion using dyes and colored water. They actually made recipes for the different potions, writing out what dyes to put in to make the different ones. There are so many things that can happen when you have water. You can even talk about what happened over the weekend. Did any of the water evaporate . . . and why?"

This was actually a very lengthy discussion. The interviewer interrupted to ask for clarification about the

75

"soothing" effect of water; and there was a long interchange about some older children the teacher had recently observed at a water table. Also, the teacher cited many more examples of measuring things than are reproduced here. What is reproduced, however, serves our illustrative purpose well.

Stephanie's initial comments about the one-inch cubes were coded in Category 3, valuable for teaching a general concept. That is, she perceived that the cubes help children understand the general notions of quantity and measurement. The remark about measuring the difference in the distance that the race cars traveled involved both measurement and subtraction. Her later remarks, however, clearly suggested a symbolic value to cubes, as the children used them for money or poker chips, or as extra materials in their building and art work. These remarks were coded in Category 1. Her discussion of the Lego set and the boy who got involved with gears illustrated the second part of the Category 2 definition, "children learn about a phenomenon from direct contact with it." Her earlier discussion of some machines she had brought into the room and the children's involvement in taking them apart also illustrated this value category.

The first value that is mentioned for water, its soothing effect, was coded in Category 4—valuable for personal/social reasons. The rest of the water discussion provides additional examples of Categories 1 and 2. Water was used symbolically when the children colored it with dye and it became a "witch's potion." One would imagine they were also learning something about dyes in the process. Water promoted general ideas about math, and it led to experimentation and inquiry into problems of siphoning and evaporation. The properties of water per se were explored when children got into the question of floating and sinking objects. The entire discussion reinforced the impression that this teacher valued materials primarily for their "many possibilities" and "experiential learning" characteristics.

It seems clear that the teacher in this vignette has received much more informational support from her observations than someone who perceived the purpose of one-inch cubes as being only for counting, or who looked upon water play (with plastic containers) as valuable only for teaching the concept of pints and quarts. Because of the greater informational support, this teacher was also able to see many connections between her comprehensive priorities for children and her surface curriculum. This, at least, is an interpretation strongly suggested by the interview data.

The coding of materials also yielded interesting results with respect to the Group 2 teachers, whose priorities were dominated by a concern for grade-level facts and skills.

GROUP 2 TEACHERS AND MATERIALS

The Group 1 teachers who were experimenting only minimally with surface curricular changes described some semistructured material in their classrooms, but they apparently did not have much environmental/natural material. The Group 2 teachers who were experimenting and who were anxious about it, however, described a fair amount of both types of material. What they tended to perceive as valuable in these materials makes the source of their anxiety even clearer.

Over 50 percent of the Group 2 responses to materials fell in Categories 5 and 6, "valuable for doing different things" and "valuable for teaching a specific outcome," with the greatest number falling in the latter category. Other categories mentioned with some frequency by these teachers were "valuable for teaching a general concept" and "valuable for motivational and managerial reasons." Only 10 percent of their remarks were coded in Categories 1 and 2.

Given a dominant priority of "grade-level facts and skills," the teaching of these *specific outcomes* by one-inch cubes or by such things as measuring how far a rabbit hops must certainly seem of questionable efficiency in these teachers' minds. (Many, in fact, alluded to just such an uneasiness.) Similarly, if the major purpose of many materials is understood only as providing children an opportunity to "do different things," then one might indeed feel uncertain about the legitimacy of their presence in the classroom. Many Group 3 teachers also saw materials as valuable for doing different things, but they frequently (if somewhat hazily) connected this value with a priority such as "initiative"— i.e., materials that lend themselves to a variety of uses provide an opportunity for children to initiate many different activities. Understandably, the Group 2 teachers found it difficult to perceive a connection between "doing different things" and "grade-level facts and skills."

THE IMPORTANCE OF SEEING CONNECTIONS

A great deal has been said thus far about seeing connections between surface curriculum and organizing priorities. Why is it important for teachers to be able to reflect upon their basic priorities and analyze connections to the ongoing activities of the classroom? Why is it important that they be able to articulate this kind of analytic reflection in an interview situation? While acknowledging the fact that people can know things and understand things in ways that cannot be verbalized, we believe that analytic reflection, and the ability to articulate it, are important in at least two respects.

First, analysis and articulation are critical components of the teacher's ability to communicate to others: to administrators, to parents, to other teachers, and, in a much more subtle and complex way, to children. This is certainly the most frequently mentioned, and widely debated, sense in which analytic articulation may be regarded as important. But second, and less commonly discussed, analytic reflection would appear to be a critical tool for the teacher's evaluation of his own efforts—especially when things start to go poorly or to stagnate. If priorities or connections are only dimly perceived, what conscious frame of reference can be brought to bear in an attempt to analyze what is going wrong? We are not advocating that a teacher should be able to formulate a rationale or purpose for everything that is done in the classroom, and we are not denying that the immediacy and complexity of teaching demands heavy reliance on common sense and intuition. The point is, can intuition later be examined in a reflective way? This ability becomes increasingly important as teachers assume greater responsiblity for curricular decisions.

CHAPTER
5

TEACHERS' UNDERSTANDINGS OF
CHILDREN

The theme of "knowing the children better" ran throughout most of the interviews. Even teachers who were quite unsure about the relevance of this information to instruction remarked that they knew more about their children than before. Although this was a recurring observation, it was most explicitly stated in response to the question: "Do you consider judging the progress of individual children to be more, or less, difficult in an informal setting?" Nine of the teachers had never taught in any way other than informally, so their responses to this question were necessarily speculative. The rest of the teachers were divided on the matter of the difficulty of judging, but they were not divided on the opinion that they knew more about children, as these comments illustrate.

"Easier in an informal setting. You see so much more."

"In the traditional mode it was easy to tick things off, but once you really start working with children it gets harder. . . . You realize there's a lot more there and you are less quick to put labels on."

"Much more difficult in the sense of record keeping. In my head I have a more accurate assessment, but it's difficult to communicate."

"In a way it's easier because you're more acutely aware of kids, but to be more aware is harder."

The second comment above also touches upon a problem that confronted many of the teachers and led to their raising several questions. How do you interpret observations? What meanings and significance can be attached to what is observed? Given more information about a child or a group of children, what do you do with it? The perplexing task of interpreting and evaluating observations was perceived as overwhelming by two or three teachers, but the majority were resolving it in one way or another. From their testimony, however, this is a difficulty that any teacher may expect to meet when he or she begins to open up a classroom to the realities of children and of child life. In fact, many portrayed it as a definite problem during their first year in the program. It should be added that the teachers also saw it as a "good problem" by frequently saying that knowing the children better was one of the satisfying and rewarding aspects of teaching in an open classroom program.

The teachers varied greatly in the qualities they ascribed to children and in their assumptions regarding the relationship of these qualities to learning and instruction. Thus, such common phrases as "knowing children better" and "knowing where a child is at" carried with them a variety of meanings because they were embedded in different construct systems. *How* teachers interpreted and evaluated their observations of children is the subject of the rest of this chapter.

QUALITIES PERCEIVED IN CHILDREN

A number of questions in the interview focused on various topics related directly to children. The analyses presented in this section deal with three general categories of perceived qualities: (1) needs and feelings, (2) interests and choice, and (3) social interaction among children. In these analyses, as in the analysis of curriculum priorities, teachers' responses throughout the entire curriculum/child section of the interview served as the basis for coding. If, for example, a teacher indicated vaguely that "children learn from each other" in response to the specific question about the benefits of small-group interaction—but did not suggest this perception in response to any of the other questions—the interview was coded as yielding little evidence of any assumptions about social interaction. None of the coding was restricted to a particular question or subset of questions.

CONSTRUCTS RELATED TO NEEDS AND FEELINGS

The first question on the topic of needs and feelings was: "Do you think that children tend to express their needs and feelings more freely in an open setting as compared with the more conventional classroom?" This was followed by additional probes concerning any difficulties or benefits for teachers and children that result from freer expression. A question was also raised about the place in the classroom of affect-laden content such as birth, death, sex, and the fears that children have.

In listening to the teachers talking about children's feelings, one is struck by the unanimity of opinion on several matters. First, every teacher, without exception, thought that the open setting did promote freer expression of feelings. In fact, many teachers so clearly indicated this belief during the opening portions of the interview that the question had to be transformed into a lead-in statement. ("You have already indicated that children tend to express their needs and feelings, but does this ever cause any difficulties for you?") Second, every teacher thought that the benefits of such expression for children outweighed the difficulties it might cause. Third, a majority of the teachers at some time during the interview, if not in response to the needs and feelings questions, made reference to the freer expression of their own feelings as well. ("I let the children know I'm human, too." "There's room for kidding and joking now." "They know I can get upset.") Fourth, almost every teacher who could compare and contrast the informal setting with a more conventional one felt that the relationship between teacher and child was now more personal, friendly, and satisfying.

Finally, although difficulties were definitely perceived in an atmosphere of more open expression, a great many teachers commented on the overall reduction in behavior problems from their previous experience. We did not probe for such a comparison, so it was by no means a unanimously voiced opinion. Nevertheless, enough teachers spontaneously offered the opinion to warrant mentioning it here.

In summary, all of the teachers believed that children's feelings had to be considered, and that a classroom which permitted greater freedom of expression was a move in the right direction. They differed noticeably, however, in the degree to which they perceived affective life to be central to classroom functioning and

and in their conception of the relationship between emotion and learning.

Table 5 shows the coding scheme that was developed to summarize the views expressed by teachers about children's needs and feelings. Teachers were checked for as many different viewpoints (in as many categories) as their pattern of remarks suggested.

Table 5

Coding Scheme: Children's Needs and Feelings

---

1. There is evidence that the teacher attempts to help children express and discuss feelings in the service of personal growth and/or emotional health.

2. There is evidence that the teacher utilizes feelings as departure points for instruction in many areas. Emotional life is viewed as relevant to cognitive growth as well as to personal mental health.

3. Emotional expression is encouraged and welcomed, but there is little evidence of its utilization in instruction.

4. There is evidence that the teacher accords legitimacy to feelings in a humanistic sense. For example: an effort is made to comfort children in distress; the teacher alters or revises instructional plans or assigned work to accommodate temporary feeling states that disrupt the child's functioning.

5. Emotional needs and feelings are generally equated with children's expressing their desires or competing for attention.

   The teacher views this as healthy.

   The teacher views this as a problem.

   The teacher views this as something that must be controlled and structured.

6. Needs and feelings are generally equated with children not being afraid to ask questions, to speak out, and to state uncertainties or confusions about their work.

7. Needs and feelings are encouraged only superficially.

8. The expression of needs, feelings, and sensitive content seems to threaten the teacher.

Our analysis yielded four patterns of coding that define differences of orientation among the teachers. These orientations are summarized in Table 6.

Table 6

Summary Results:

Orientation of Teachers to
Children's Emotional Needs and Feelings

Orientation	Dominant Coding Category	Subsidiary Coding Categories	Percentage of Total Group (N=60)
A. Needs and feelings are only remotely perceived and lack reality.	7	6, 8	20
B. Needs and feelings are perceived as real and their expression as desirable, but they are also seen to be in conflict with learning.	5	4, 6, 8	15
C. The expression of needs and feelings is seen as a necessary context for learning.	3, 4	-	32
D. The expression of needs and feelings is seen as integral to and inseparable from the learning process.	1, 2	-	33

Orientation A (20%). In Orientation A, the reality of children's needs and feelings was only remotely perceived, and little encouragement was apparently given to the children's expression of feeling. The relevance of emotional life to instruction was for the most part either ignored or denied. For some of these teachers the main benefit of a more open atmosphere, beyond its being more pleasant and relaxed, was that the children were not afraid or hesitant to speak out and state their confusion about an assignment. This was generally discussed as a benefit to the teacher in knowing how to proceed with instruction. It was rarely articulated as a benefit from the child's perspective. In fact, the only time a child's viewpoint was mentioned by this group was in response to the question about disruptive influences in the classroom. Here, several teachers did speculate about possible reasons for the continual disruptive behavior of a particular child and attempted to consider the child's perspective and how he must feel to act the way he did. It was as if only an extreme form of behavior brought the child into focus as a person with needs and feelings. Occasionally, some of these teachers hinted that too much free expression might be threatening.

Orientation B (15%). A second orientation is best characterized as ambivalent, equating needs and feelings with "problems." In contrast to the first pattern, this orientation was more complex and conveyed a strong sense of the reality of children's affective life. There was a conviction that it is good for a child to be able to express his worries or misunderstandings to the teacher, just as it is important for him to work through relationships with peers. But there was also a marked ambivalence about the teacher's role in coping with or responding to feelings, arguments, or bids for attention.

> "I am cut up into 30 pieces. I want to meet every child's needs, but I can't. The children continually want attention, even those who seem most independent. . . . They come over and tell me personal stories."

> "Children say things more openly, like: 'I don't want to do that.' I'm sometimes not sure how to respond."

> "By allowing this openness, you also allow true personalities you might not see otherwise, and you get into the problem of working with these personalities. We have more problems because of this openness. . . . It gives you more problems to help solve and try to find the answers."

> "There's a boy obsessed with things of a sexual nature, and it keeps coming out in his clay and painting."

These teachers also saw the positive side of children's feelings, as they commented on the expression of joy, on the telling of jokes, on the intensity of friendships. Here again, however, there was a sense of concern about controlling or meeting the expression of such affect. ("They sometimes get too excited." "That's why we had to change the doll house to a store.")

In summary, the characteristic ambivalence of this orientation was marked by a belief in the importance and reality of children's feelings, but also by the assumption that the expression of these feelings must somehow be coped with or controlled if learning is to proceed. A child can't learn if he is "upset," "too excited," or even "too interested." The affective life was viewed as almost at odds with the cognitive.

Orientation C (32%). Orientation C teachers perceived the expression of needs and feelings to be a natural condition, and they welcomed such expression for its contribution to the creation of a warm and humane environment in which learning could take place.

> "I hated the older way, because children just sat all morning—they couldn't move around and talk. How could they learn!"

> "It's a much better way to learn. . . . It's only natural."

> "They love school now. They hate to leave in the afternoon. If they get upset, they know that the teacher will listen or that their friends will help them. They have a good attitude about school."

Other teachers characterized by this orientation did not necessarily connect freer expression with the child's love of school or ability to learn. Rather, they saw it as a desirable context for development in a more general sense.

> "Children say what they think, and they're healthier for it."

> "Kids always have a need to express themselves, regardless of the classroom. But a great deal more comes up in an open classroom. There are more fights, and that disturbs me, but more good things come out too. Kids are nasty to each other, and they are very good to each other."

Orientation D (33%). Teachers who held the fourth orientation shared these concerns for a humane environment, but they were much more explicit in relating the feelings and emotions of children to their learning and development. Most often there was an emphasis on the significance of expressing feelings for the child's personal and social growth, although connections to the child's cognitive development are also evident. One teacher, for instance, had commented at several points during the interview about a snake that had been in the classroom, emphasizing how much the children loved it and had learned from it—reading about reptiles, writing stories about it, observing its habits, making different cages for it. During the discussion of feelings, the teacher related that the snake had recently escaped from its cage over a weekend and had been flushed down the toilet by one of the custodial staff. She continued:

> Actually he [the head custodian] told a child in another class who knew we had been searching for a snake. So the

child came in and announced to the class that the snake had been flushed down the toilet. Everybody was *very* upset. What a terrible thing to do! Then two children went to the custodian to find out why he had done that. He said someone had found the snake loose in the room he was cleaning, and this person was petrified of snakes so he took it and flushed it down the toilet. So then we talked about fears that people have and how sometimes you act unnecessarily . . . and they began to understand a lot of things."

A kindergarten teacher was most articulate in response to the question about any difficulties that an open expression of feelings caused for the teacher :

"It's an important problem. When children are in a situation where you're not dealing with feelings, they just push them down. But when they can express them, you have to think what mental health really is. This is where the openness of the teacher becomes important, because what you accept in yourself you generally accept in others. Placing standards on intellectual achievement is very easy, but placing standards on someone else's emotional life is very difficult, if not impossible. So you have to go with your own acceptance. It's one of the most important aspects of this program, and it's especially important in kindergarten. If a child's feelings can stay alive and open and be dealt with at this age, and can be kept alive throughout, then you won't have the process that's happened in the past. Like you go all the way through school with closed feelings, and then when you graduate from college you can open up again—and you wonder: What are my real feelings?"

In summary, the comments of this fourth group of teachers depict the child's affective life as clearly associated with changing conceptions of himself and others and, to a certain extent, with his growing understanding of the world. An integration of thought and feeling is implied in this orientation. Such integration is not as evident in the third and second viewpoints, in which a child's emotional life is seen as either coexisting with his cognitive life, or often at odds with it.

CONSTRUCTS RELATED TO INTERESTS AND CHOICE

Learning that is shaped by children's interests and by their pursuit of interests in various activities is a core conception of the philosophy of open education. It is also a complex conception.

Interests, choice, and learning are viewed as integrally related, so that it is impossible to talk about one without implying or including the others. This fusion of interests, choice, and learning is illustrated in the following representative passages.

> The environment we seek to create within the school is one which is truly responsive to the needs and interests of children; in which children's learning is deeply rooted in experience; where knowledge becomes important because it is relevant and put to use.... (Armington, 1968, p. 7)

> I speak of the language of action . . . because it is also, and almost synonymously, the language of choice. We choose as we act, we act as we choose. . . . Not only those who teach are concerned with the way in which learning is coupled to choice, active choice. Philosophers, psychologists, and psychotherapists bring special insights which those of us in schools can use. . . . But it is the teacher who must provide the material from which choices are to be made in the classroom. (F.P. Hawkins, 1974, pp. xiv-xv)

This concern with interests and choice is not based on the assumption that children "should do what they want to do," nor is it based exclusively on child development theory. Rather, the concern stems from the educational priorities of promoting intention and purposefulness in children and of fostering the active construction, as opposed to the passive absorption, of knowledge.

> The teacher's role in informal education could be summed up as *implementing and opening up a child's* purposes. (p. 109) . . . Support for the *continuity* of a child's spiraling insights would focus on . . . the points that have meaning for a child—*his own questions* that he asks in his own developmental groping for understanding of reality. A child extends his understanding through pursuing *these* questions: he is helped to further extension if the teacher goes along *his* path, posing new possibilities. . . . (Weber, 1971, p. 194)

Within the general literature of education and psychology, however, there are many differing conceptions of choice and interest and a variety of opinions regarding their significance for teaching and learning. In one conception, sometimes identified as an open education position, choice is equated with the initial act of selecting something to do. Thus, once the child elects to work with clay, that is the end of choice. There is little concern for observing what he chooses to *do with the clay*, which is the more critical point because it reflects the ongoing expression of his interest. Choice is seen as a succession of periodic "opting-to-work-with-something" actions. In such a conception, the ability to choose may be depicted as a desirable "process outcome" of education, essentially separated from the content of learning.

In another conception, interests and choice are seen primarily as expressions of affect—the child selects what attracts him or entertains him. The privilege of choosing something of interest may also be viewed as a major motivating and reinforcing agent, and so choice and interests become something to be manipulated in the service of learning.

Given these different conceptions, there is little wonder that teachers in the study also conveyed a wide range of meanings in their use of the terms *interests* and *choice*. These topics came up early in the interview, but they were raised more explicitly by the following questions:

> You hear a lot about "building on children's interest" in an open philosophy of education—but how does this work out in practice? How do you go about utilizing or building on a child's interests? Can you give me some concrete examples?

> "Opening up" a classroom usually means giving children some amount of choice in what they do. In your experience, how do young children handle choice situations? Can they make choices? On what basis do they choose?

The question on interest was followed by a probe inquiring how the teacher dealt with children who "show little apparent interest in anything that you have in the room" or who "can't settle down and get involved." The question on choice was followed by three probes concerning (1) perceived reasons why some children could not handle choice or make purposeful choices (if that was the teacher's perception), (2) how the teacher helped children who had difficulty in choosing, and (3) how the teacher felt about children who persistently stuck to one or two activities.

Three coding schemes were developed for analyzing the teacher's thoughts about interests, choice, and learning. These are presented in Tables 7, 8, and 9. In coding the assumptions regarding children's interest, as many categories were checked as were clearly evident in a teacher's remarks. With assumptions regarding choice, we attempted to summarize the teacher's position by placing each person in one category only. However, we made a note of comments that revealed aspects of other category descriptions. For assumptions regarding worthwhile learning, the teacher's position was also summarized by a single category.

Table 7

Coding Scheme: Assumptions Regarding Interests

1. Interests have continuity—a past and a future—and are developed over time. They are not generally capricious or whimsical.

2. Interests are optimal organizers of learning. Children "connect" to phenomena in meaningful ways. They ask their own questions of phenomena, they experiment, and they construct or invent hypotheses about phenomena.

3. Interests are optimal sustainers of learning, in the sense of internal competency motivation. There is a personal investment in learning activities. Children are working primarily for themselves and not to please others.

4. Interest inherently resides in a certain material and "attracts" the child, rather than the child's investing the material with his own interest. Therefore "interesting materials" are viewed as an external motivating force that initiates and sustains the child's activity.

5. Interests make learning more enjoyable because children are more enthusiastic. The classroom is more "interesting."

6. The teacher has not given much thought to the quality of interest as it supports learning.

Table 8

Coding Scheme: Assumptions Regarding Choice

1. The focus of remarks is on the act of choosing as it relates to learning and development. Choosing is viewed as a condition necessary to the connection of interest and learning. The child's interests and capabilities give shape to learning through the process of choice. This process is also viewed as promoting a sense of purpose and intention within the child.

2. The focus of remarks is on providing activities and materials for choice, with the emphasis on their motivational or reinforcement value. The option of choosing may also be viewed as a contract between the teacher and the child, to ensure a responsibility on the child's part for carrying through with an activity.

89

3. The focus of remarks is on providing for choice as selection: the child may choose an activity, or he may ask for a material to work with. This is seen as establishing a happier and healthier atmosphere. Often, these teachers indicated that they set aside certain periods during the day as times for choice.

4. Choice is viewed as an incidental aspect of teaching and learning. Choice as such is not salient to the teacher and is restricted to minor activities.

Table 9

Coding Scheme:

Evidence of Confidence
That Worthwhile Learning Can Occur When Children Engage in
Basically Self-defined and Self-directed Activity

---

1. Clear evidence of confidence across all curricular areas:

    A discriminating perception: worthwhile learning is not assumed to be automatic. Children may also engage in coping and defensive behavior. Also, all activities are not assumed to be of uniform value and quality with respect to content and depth.

    An indiscriminant perception: the teacher apparently assumes that worthwhile learning is virtually guaranteed.

2. Evidence of ambivalence or confusion more than confidence. The teacher thinks that children are learning, but "can't always see it." Or the teacher believes this can happen, but is somewhat ambivalent about his or her ability to bring it about. The assumption of worthwhileness is held across all curricular areas.

3. Evidence of confidence that worthwhile learning can occur, but with definite qualifications. These qualifications frequently specify the particular children who are capable of learning in this way ("the mature ones"), or the particular subject areas that are conducive to such learning. Another typical qualification is the value that is placed on such learning. The teacher may view it as "extra enrichment," but definitely subordinate to basic learning in reading and math.

4. Little or no evidence of confidence that worthwhile learning occurs when children engage in self-defined and self-directed activity. Such activity is viewed mainly as "play," or as valuable for managerial reasons, such as keeping the children occupied while the teacher works with small groups.

When these schemes were analyzed in combination, four recurring patterns of coding emerged that again can be used to describe differing orientations or construct systems among the teachers. In Table 10, each of these general orientations is shown and defined by its characteristic coding pattern.

Table 10

Summary Results:

Coding Patterns of Teachers With Different Orientations Regarding Interests, Choice, and Worthwhile Learning That Occurs When Children Work Independently
(Subsidiary Codings Are Indicated in Parentheses)

Orientation	Interest Code	Choice Code	Worthwhile Learning Code
A	6	4 (3)	4
B	5 (4)	3	3
C	4 (3) (5)	2 (3)	2
D	1, 2, 3	1	1 (2)

Orientation A (20%). Teachers within this orientation were unlikely to talk much about children's interests or choices except when they responded to the specific questions about these topics. Most of them equated interests with what "children-in-general" like to do, in a rather stereotypic manner; that is, boys are interested in science and girls are interested in reading. Although the interest of an individual child was sometimes discussed, the questions on interest and choice were usually answered by reference to the propensities of a group.

"Depends on the class you get."

"Holidays are easy [for building on interest]—all children love holidays."

"This year's class loves science; last year's loved writing."

91

Individual interests that ranged outside these teachers' conceptions of curriculum were generally viewed as sporadic or whimsical.

> "Children have short-lived interests. They get involved, then drop it. They get bored."

The opportunity for children to choose activities was clearly restricted to special times of the day or by the prerequisite of getting their work done first. For some teachers, allowing children to choose was restricted to only very minor activities, or it was viewed as a strategy for keeping children occupied while the teacher worked with small groups. In summary, the interests of children and their capacity to choose were seen as weak and unreliable resources for learning, and so these "resources" carried few implications for instruction. A few teachers within this orientation openly acknowledged the difference between their views and the philosophy of the open education program they were in.

> "That's another problem I have. The program provided all these nice materials, but I can't use them. I have Harper and Row to cover and a math series to cover. . . . The children use the materials when they have time, but I don't have time to use them."

> "We have a prescribed curriculum, and we have to cover certain areas. We're not free to go with children's interests all the time. Last week I had a unit on Japan, and the children wanted to make a lantern—which was O.K. We can go beyond areas."

Orientation B (30%). Although there was considerable variation within this second orientation, the teachers composing it shared two characteristic beliefs. First, they believed that worthwhile learning did occur when children pursued their interests in activities, but this was regarded as "enrichment" or "additional learning." Not one of these teachers thought of children's interests as being directly connected with learning in reading and mathematics—areas they perceived to be the basics of their curriculum, or at least areas where they were responsible for children's performance at grade-level expectancy. Some of these teachers tried to make mathematics and reading more interesting for children by using what they perceived to be more interesting materials or activities, but they did not see children's interests as resources for such learning, and they did not permit choice with respect to these areas.

Occasionally, teachers also stressed the need "to meet" or "to satisfy" children's interests. Thus, some vacillated between seeing interests as an impetus to learning and seeing them as natural desires or dynamic needs that must somehow be permitted expression and gratification. ("They have to get it out of their system.")

A second perception shared by this group centered on the vitality of interests. Activities and projects were definitely liked or disliked by children; and what they liked, they "thoroughly enjoyed." In this sense, the expression of interest was perceived as virtually synonymous with the expression of positive affect. The teachers valued choice and the opportunity to work from interests primarily for the satisfaction that choice and interests brought to the children, but also for the happier, "more interesting" environment that they created for teachers and children alike. ("All the different things we do are fun.")

In their concentration on the pleasure of working with children in a more open setting, however, these teachers tended not to see the puzzlement, frustration, and perseverance that children also display when they attempt to work through an idea. The lack of such a perception in these teachers' accounts was probably due to the fact that they, like teachers of Orientation A, generally thought of interests as propensities of children. Thus, one principal way in which they "built on interests" was to create a large group project out of the interests of one or two children.

> "The children will bring in something, and we will decide to do a unit on this because you decide the children are interested in it. One child brought in postcards from her trip, and this started a whole thing on where people travel."

> "When the astronauts landed on the moon, a couple of boys were *really* interested, and we started to build a spaceship. It was really a large and intricate thing, and all the children loved working on it. They all got excited about the astronauts."

Although most of their remarks focused on group characteristics, many of these teachers revealed a sharpened perception of individual children's interests, or the breaking down of stereotypes and of preconceived expectations.

> "You know, children really are interested in all kinds of things. They bring in broken machines, boxes, turtles, and . . . well, things I just wouldn't have imagined."

93

"I've observed that interests aren't actually divided between boys and girls. Usually, I thought girls would not be interested in planes, but they all got just as involved with that spaceship as the boys. And when we were crocheting, the boys really got excited about crocheting belts. Maybe you don't believe that. I wouldn't have before—but it's *really true!*"

"Some of the so-called interest areas, like the dress-up corner, are not necessarily interesting to children."

With respect to choice, most of these teachers believed that children could handle the problem of selection rather well, but it was obvious that they generally interpreted choice as "selection." ("When given the opportunity, they usually find something to do that interests them.") They also made it clear, however, that the children had definite assigned work in reading and mathematics that had to be completed. Some made daily assignments; some made assignments covering a week's period. Aside from these similarities, they varied greatly in how they handled the matter of choice. Some teachers were like the Orientation A group in that they required the assigned work to be completed before children could select other activities. Unlike the A teachers, however, they made sure to leave a reasonable length of time for choice activities—either the entire afternoon or a large part of it. Other teachers preferred to have the choice activities in the morning, when the children were "fresh" and had "a lot of energy to work off." Still others provided for choice activities and work assignments to go on simultaneously. That is, the children could choose when they wanted to do their assigned work and when they wanted to work on other group or individual projects.

Orientation C (22%). The assumptions that constitute Orientation C differ from those of Orientation B in two major respects. These teachers analyzed interest and choice in terms of individual patterns rather than group propensities, and they sensed a definite connection between children's expression of interest and their investigative learning in reading and mathematics as well as in other basic areas of the curriculum. In general, these teachers were much more aware of the variety and strength of interests represented in their classrooms.

Unlike the teachers of Orientation D, however, this group tended to perceive interests as more manipulable by the teacher and more easily influenced by external stimuli such as peer opinion or the attractiveness of materials.

"I create interest more than build on it . . . . You put out things, initiate interest. Also, children will copy each other, and this leads to projects."

"I try to use what they bring in, but there are a lot of teacher-set projects too. With the seven-year-olds, though, it's easier to work on non-teacher-directed activities because there's lots of peer influence."

Perhaps the most important, but subtle, distinction between the thinking of teachers in this group and those who are characterized as Orientation D is that they generally accepted the expression of interests at face value. If a child brings in a shell, for example, this means he is interested in shells or, possibly, the seashore. Such literal interpretation leads to trips to the library to obtain books on shells and sea life, to a display of shells, or to the classification of shells. It tends not to lead to making shell jewelry or to the raising of snails.

"If a child brings in something, a butterfly for instance, I do try to have them go up to the library and take out all the books they can find on the subject (or else I do it) and get out the microscope, or something to this effect. Or, if a child brings in a lot of shavings or packing material, I set them on the art table and ask what we can do with this. Some children show an interest in bringing books from home to read. Fine . . . bring those in. Same with math. A little girl brought in an adding machine and learned how to add with it."

"There was a boy interested in dinosaurs, so I first helped him make a book. He would draw pictures and then write something about each kind—the Brontosaurus and so on. Then I brought in lots of books about dinosaurs for him to read. . . It's a good approach for children who have trouble with reading."

When an expression of interest is consistently interpreted at face value, the teacher will miss the range of meanings it may hold for a child and will have difficulty in conceiving of the many directions in which the interest can be developed. Bringing in a butterfly, for example, may represent an interest in butterflies; but it may also represent an interest in things that fly, an interest in things that seem to "float on the wind," an interest in color and design, or an interest in sharing something with others. The teachers who had this orientation, however, interpreted the initial topic of interest as an indication that the child wished to study that topic in its own right—a study of butterflies or dinosaurs.

95

They also tended to use this interest to advance a child's skills in reading and mathematics (measuring the purported length of dinosaurs was a familiar example). In appraising the possibilities of an interest, they tended to focus on *what* the child was interested in, not on *why* he was interested in it. Because of this characteristic tendency, many teachers found it difficult to consider how certain interests might lead to worthwhile learning experiences.

> "Some interests like drumming . . . I just can't see where it could go academically."

> "He keeps bringing in birds' nests. They're filling a shelf and I don't know what we can do with them."

On the question of choice, many of these teachers emphasized the importance of carry-through and responsibility once the child had made a selection. Some children were viewed as handling this well, others as handling it less well. The latter were frequently described as somewhat immature or unmotivated, or as coming from over-protective homes and hence unable to make up their minds.

> "Most children in the second year of the program are able to choose. To get them to make wise decisions is more of a challenge. During the week they should get to most areas of the room. . . . They have to produce, too, once in an area."

> "Some are motivated and independent enough to pursue activities. Others need direction and you tell them they must pick one of these three and finish it."

> "They can't just dabble. . . ."

Thus, choice was seen as a privilege of selection and a responsibility to carry out the activity to a productive end. Unlike Orientation B teachers, these Orientation C teachers were not simply concerned with the initial selection a child made. But unlike Orientation D teachers, they did not construe choosing as ongoing—as part of the process that leads to an "end product."

In summary, these teachers perceived that being interested in something was much more than enjoyment. They seemed greatly concerned with establishing a connection between the child's interests and the content of the curriculum, but there was often an uneasy balance between their own curricular goals and the interests they perceived in children. In one way or another, they acknowledged that teaching and learning were not the same, and they perceived the validity of interests. On the other hand, they lacked confidence in the validity of pursuing some interests and/or in their own ability to turn interests to productive purposes. Many teachers articulated their perplexity.

> "I feel I can't depend on their interests alone, however, because something doesn't always come up each day that would make a worthwhile learning experience."

> "This is my lack [building on interests]. When I can build, we can go so very far . . . but, for instance, there's one child with a *great* interest in our greenhouse, but *no* interest in reading or mathematics. [pause] We teachers need much more help and work on this."

> "Some kids, you try a hundred things and can't find what they're interested in. For others, it's easy.

> "Sometimes I say, 'If you can't find something in the next few minutes, then I'm going to have to sit down and we're going to find something for you for the rest of the day.' I'm not pleased with that approach. I would like them to come up with something on their own."

Orientation D (28%). A viewpoint common to teachers of Orientations B and C was that children, by nature, are interested and curious, and that such interests have a place in the school. Although interests were interpreted differently within each orientation, both B and C teachers tended to see a wide range of individual differences in the ability of children to "have interests." This was not true of Orientation D teachers. The assumption that interest is a quality of *all* children, and that there is continuity and strength in children's interests, clearly characterized this orientation.

> "Children always have interests. There's no such thing as a child not utilizing time."

> "Kids are nice that way. If you miss an interest the first time, they just keep doing things to tell you about it, until it finally hits you what the interest is."

This assumption of the universality and resilience of interests was perhaps most evident in responses given to the probes: "What about children who show little interest, who can't seem to get involved?" and "How do you help children who have difficulty choosing?" Teachers of Orientation D generally responded to these probes by considering that a child might be shy or cautious, or that something in the situation might be holding him back. They did not assume that children lacked interests.

"A shy child might simply have to get to know you well enough—to know you'll support her."

"Sometimes the children choose at random, but mostly they don't. When a child can't choose, it's sometimes because the choices are too abstract, and he can't tune in or get a handle on it. Or sometimes, the child's interests are simply in conflict with what I have put out."

"I think three things influence the child who 'flits' or is just 'floating around.' First, it may be a bad day, and then you sit down and talk about the problem. Or, it may be unfamiliarity with the materials. I usually discuss new things in a class meeting, but some children need further discussion. And sometimes the child's real interest is not represented in the choices for the day. Then you have to help that child find or get out more appropriate materials. . . . The teacher's role is really critical here."

"Usually it's children who have little pride in what they do [who can't get involved]. You try to catch them in the middle of their two- or three-minute thing and show them there's something of potential value in it. For example, I managed to catch a child like this who had just painted three or four strokes and was about to leave. I added a stroke and asked her about the others . . . just to show I was interested. The question is *why* children do this. Sometimes it's an attention span problem, but usually it's a need to see that their work can have value—that they can do something."

Also apparent in these teachers' comments was the assumption that it is possible to bring out and to "connect with" a child's interests through the processes of observation and inquiry. Teaching was not regarded as a matter of creating interests in children, but of identifying and stimulating interests.

"If you say, 'I can't interest him in anything,' then you are assuming that you have to make an interest in the child. That's not the issue. You have to observe and find out about him."

Teachers of Orientation D depicted children's interests as integral to learning. Interests led to investigations that took a variety of directions and that were characterized by intent and purpose. Unlike group C, these teachers did not interpret an initial expression of interest at face value. They were very much concerned with the way in which children chose to investigate a particular matter, evaluating their choices along the way as indicating the real direction of their interests. Thus, these teachers did not focus only on the child's initial selection of something to work with or only the end-product of his efforts. Similarly, interests were not perceived as needing to be satisfied and therefore resolved. The challenge was not to "meet" or "satisfy" interests, but to promote their expression and realization in worthwhile learning.

"A girl saw her tracks in the snow in the playground. Then she and some others looked at car tracks—and then at some tracks in the dirt. Three children got very involved and made plaster of Paris tracks. . . ."

"We had these milk boxes out in the playground—plastic ones, steel ones, and wooden ones. The kids started sliding down the slides in them . . . and then we noticed they were really curious about how fast each kind would go and how far, so we started measuring. We didn't make a big math thing out of it, we just measured and had the strings hung up in the corridor—yellow strings for the wooden boxes, red for the steel ones, and blue for the plastic. Then we hit on the idea of how they'd travel on different surfaces. We put out wet sand, dry sand, wet leaves, and in the winter it was ice. Again, we didn't get into physics formally, but most of them got the idea of surfaces and of friction."

"One day, four children got this 'thing' about getting on chairs and pushing them around the room—they called themselves the 'Flyers Club.' Then I made a sign, 'Flyers Club,' with each one's name on it. We talked about where each one wanted to go, and then they wrote about where they were going. After a while, this led to getting out the map and seeing where the different places were, and they got interested in how maps are made and what they tell you. Then they finally ended up making an airplane. . . . It was a real lesson for me that you can turn things that seem as if they're going to be chaotic into constructive directions that have relevance for children. Teachers have to learn that they can use their planning and organizational ability for something that comes up on-the-spot, and not always for preconceived things you think children will do."

These examples also convey a picture of the active role of the teacher. Orientation D teachers were not only concerned with identifying interests, but, equally important, with promoting their extension. As can be surmised, the ways they described of extending interests were as varied as the projects themselves. "Extending interests," for these teachers, meant finding more and more points of connection between a child's interests and the content of the classroom.

Although Orientation D teachers shared a belief about the importance of building on interests, more than half of them also discussed the difficulty of this task.

> "This is most difficult. I feel least successful here. It boils down to listening hard . . . letting kids know you really mean it. It's important that you honor what they want to do, but the new ideas too often come from me. I would like more to come from them."

> "I get the feeling of not being able to keep up. . . . I feel I haven't taken things nearly as far as possible."

> "It's not easy to pick up on everything children bring in. For instance, I can't extend doll play. I let them take their dolls to the gym, but for the most part I ask them to put the dolls away in the classroom, because I just don't know what to do with them."

In responding to specific questions about choice, there was very little mention by these teachers of the problem of getting children to carry through with what they had chosen to do. Instead, the discussion of problems tended to focus more on helping children make good choices, on helping a particular child develop a sense of his own interests, or on the validity of children opting *not* to extend an interest.

> "Sometimes you think you're going to pick up on an interest, and the child really doesn't want to extend it. He likes it just for what it is. [A lengthy example of a boy interested in planets.] I think you have to respect that desire on the child's part too."

> "I am concerned about kids who won't touch certain areas . . . won't get involved with animals, magic powders, the plants. I would like them to try themselves in different areas."

100

"It does concern me if a child doesn't feel free to choose another activity . . . or if he's just playing safe with something he knows he likes."

In summary, when teachers in this group used such phrases as "it's important for children to do what interests them," they brought to that statement a conception of interest and choice that was different from that of teachers who had other orientations. Children's pursuit of interests was perceived as a process of investigation, experimentation, and construction, with purpose and intent on the child's part. Within the group, teachers differed mainly in the degree to which they perceived that they had been successful in promoting such learning in the classroom. All of them, however, believed they had much more to learn.

CONSTRUCTS RELATED TO RECIPROCITY AND SOCIAL INTERACTION

Reciprocity in human relationships is such a pervasive fact of experience that its contribution to learning is often overlooked. Not only is it overlooked; it has been denied by many forms of traditional education in which one criterion of good teaching is the "quietness of the classroom."

Reciprocity means that we learn from each other. We reconstruct, reinforce, or refine our thinking on the basis, and in the process, of interacting with other people. Although common sense suggests the importance of a child's interaction with adults, peer interaction is also crucial. The function of peer interaction in promoting intellectual development is perhaps more easily demonstrated in adult life. It is almost impossible, for example, to conceive of growth in a job where communication about work is prohibited. While this is an obvious enough fact, many adults seem to have given little thought to the role of reciprocity in children's intellectual development. A similar neglect exists in the general educational literature.

Reciprocity also leads to learning about oneself and other people; and it is here, in the area of personal and social growth, that most adults recognize the importance of peer interaction for children. Often, however, such learning is thought to be best relegated to "after school hours" or "during recess."

The effect of relegating children's social interaction to "off-classroom limits" is to ignore the opportunity of guiding this pervasive influence into constructive learning. Peer learning is powerful and it can work to any end, not all of them necessarily beneficial. Just as peer influence can serve to contribute to variety and breadth in learning, so also it can restrict choice and dampen unpopular interests. The solution is not to cut off this resource for learning, but to encourage it and guide it.

Within open education philosophy, peer interaction is considered intrinsic to learning—cognitive, as well as personal and social. Reciprocity is regarded as a prime educative process in and of itself. As Susan Isaacs has put it:

> If we deprive him of free speech with his fellows, we take away from him one of the most valuable means of intellectual and social growth. (1965, p. 153)

> It is not the mere presence of other children but active participation with them, doing real things together, an active interchange of feeling and experience, which educates the child. (1948, p. 226)

Piaget (1973) is emphatic in his discussion of peer interaction and reciprocity:

> No real intellectual activity could be carried on in the form of experimental actions and spontaneous investigations without free collaboration among individuals—that is to say, among students themselves, and not only between the teacher and the student. (pp. 108-109)

He goes on to say that putting one's intellect to work requires not only the back-and-forth of mutual stimulation, but also the mutual exercise of considered opinion and critical judgment.

Teachers in the study discussed social interaction most directly in response to the question: "In an open setting children often work in small groups. What benefits do you see in such small groupings?" A particularly interesting feature of this question was the characteristic manner in which teachers chose to respond to it. Some assumed that the interviewer meant benefits for the teacher in working with small groups. Others reacted to the question with the assumption that the interviewer was referring to children working together by themselves, without direct teacher supervision. This latter group responded either with what benefits they perceived for children in such a setting, what benefits they perceived for the teacher, or what benefits they perceived for both.

These different interpretations of the question—interpretations about the teacher's presence in or absence from the group and about who was benefiting from the situation—reflected, in turn, the teacher's general position within a broad spectrum of assumptions and opinions regarding social interaction. Thus, one teacher responding with a teacher-absent assumption stressed again and again throughout the interview that the "key" to running an open classroom resides in children working together in a socially cohesive manner. These remarks were not directed to classroom management problems as much as they were to the critical importance of children's tapping each other's resources. ("If you don't have that in the classroom, forget it!") In contrast, a teacher who responded with the teacher-present assumption viewed open education primarily as individualized instruction and emphasized the need to have several adults in the classroom in order to "really individualize." Small groups, for her, represented a more efficient way in which adults could direct the ebb and flow of learning. The former teacher welcomed adults also, but, consistent with her priorities, she qualified this view by noting that too many adults could retard the development of working relationships among the children.

The coding scheme for summarizing dominant perspectives on children's social interaction is presented in Table 11. The working distinction between the first two categories of this scheme, the "reciprocity categories," and categories 3 and 4 will be taken up in the discussion of different orientations. The coding patterns that emerged in analysis and the different orientations they reflect are presented in Table 12.

Table 11

Coding Scheme: Children's Social Interaction

---

1. Interaction is viewed in terms of reciprocity and considered essential for cognitive growth.

2. Interaction is viewed in terms of reciprocity and considered essential for personal-social growth.

3. Children are perceived as learning from each other cognitively, but the emphasis is on one child "instructing" another about specific concepts, or showing him how to do a specific task.

4. Children are perceived as learning from each other in a personal-social sense, but the emphasis is on social norms of behavior—learning how to cooperate, sharing responsibilities, sharing materials.

5. Interaction is viewed as creating a more natural and sociable atmosphere.

6. Interaction is viewed as potentially disruptive. It must be controlled and structured or it will interfere with learning.

7. There is little evidence that interaction is viewed as valuable for cognitive learning. Instead, the emphasis is on individualized instruction of a one-to-one nature, the child either interacting directly with the teacher or with some material.

8. There is little evidence of any assumptions regarding children's interaction.

Table 12

Summary Results: Children's Social Interaction

Orientation	Dominant Coding Category	Subsidiary Coding Categories	Percentage of Total Group (N=60)
A. Interaction generally not perceived as significant for learning.	8	7	18
B. Interaction perceived as potentially interfering with learning.	6	3, 5	5
C. Interaction perceived as children "instructing" one another or as learning socially accepted norms.	3, 4	5	37
D. Interaction perceived as reciprocity, as a process of learning—either cognitive, or personal-social, or both.	1, 2	3, 5	40

Orientation A (18%). Teachers in Orientation A did not appear to perceive peer interaction either as an educative process or as a significant resource for children helping one another. In response to the question on small groups, they tended to dwell mainly on the benefits for the teacher: "You can find out about each child"; "You're able to individualize." Unlike teachers of other orientations, they were not likely to comment on the kinds of things that children can learn from each other. When benefits for the children were considered or probed for, they were benefits relating to a child's feelings and not to the process of interaction.

> "Shy children would not like to recite in front of the whole class."

> "Nobody feels funny about not getting [i.e., understanding] something."

For some, the very process of interaction itself was seen as something that had to be instilled by the teacher. Thus, instead of a process to be built on or worked with, interaction was cast as a character trait, with some children having learned more of it than others.

> "We have to learn to help each other. We have to learn to work with each other."

Orientation B (5%). The small group of Orientation B teachers could perceive possibilities for learning in interaction. However, they were so focused on the disruptive or interfering qualities of interaction that they conveyed ambivalence and an uncertain and inconsistent viewpoint. They believed that children were "better off" when they could work more openly with one another—that they enjoyed working together and could teach each other—but these perceptions were subsidiary to the concern they voiced about the hazards of interaction and the continual need to channel it into appropriate directions. In contrast to most of the Orientation A teachers, all of these teachers had apparently worked a great deal on expanding their surface curriculum, and they actively promoted exchange among children. They did not appear to regret these actions or to want to reverse them, but they did dwell on management problems which they perceived as almost inherent in an informal classroom.

> "Children can help each other when sometimes I don't realize they need help. Of course, in helping they also copy each other. I've discussed that with them."

> "Friends work best together, but they can get too much off on their own."

"There's an awful lot of fooling around, but you have to expect some of that."

Orientation C (37%). Teachers in the Orientation C group were more consistent and more convinced in their beliefs about the significance of social interaction for instruction. They saw such interaction as leading to the learning of ideas and skills and as related to children's developing sense of responsibility and community. When they contrasted their current views with previous ideas, they found in children's working together a tremendous resource for instruction that previously had not been tapped nor even considered.

What distinguished this group from Orientation D teachers is that they tended to perceive learning, particularly cognitive learning, as didactic in nature. They tended not to characterize the learning process itself as interactive. Thus, about three-fourths of the group stressed the fact that children were very capable of helping one another with classroom work and with projects. A recurrent theme was "children can be very good teachers."

"I never realized how much kids could teach each other."

"Children do much of my teaching now. My skill work is individualized, but the kids help one another a great deal."

"They learn from each other. Second graders learn from third graders and vice versa."

"A child that's good will help someone who's not doing as well. The really good one won't give the other the answer . . . but will have them sound out the words. . . ."

As these remarks imply, children learning from each other is conceived more as a one-directional process than as exchange or reciprocity. One child is perceived as the more or less passive benefactor of another child's knowledge. In part, this perception reflects the fact that much of the content of the depicted interaction was the content of the established curriculum and not the content of the children's ideas and capabilities. But there were exceptions to this, as indicated when teachers perceived the sharing of special qualities and abilities.

"One girl is very good in art. The kids get lots of ideas from her . . . which they could never get from me. I'm terrible in art."

"The Spanish-speaking children learn English . . . and the others learn some Spanish."

106

A few noted that they originally believed children would only copy each other but had discovered that children knew the distinction between helping one another and "doing someone else's work." This distinction was considered important, not only for the children, but as a point to be communicated to parents who were not accustomed to thinking of learning in these terms.

Many of these teachers also thought that working together promoted a more sociable atmosphere, enjoyed by children and teacher alike. Some, however, indicated a degree of uneasiness about the place of "fun" in the classroom and made a point of telling the interviewer that the children *learn* as well as have fun.

> "Working together is part of my program . . . and even though it's fun, they still have to learn."

The majority of the group emphasized the significance of interaction for the children's developing sense of responsibility and respect for each other. When the children shared the managerial responsibilities of the classroom—cleaning up, caring for animals, organizing activities—the teachers saw that children could learn in a first-hand way about the necessities and rewards of interdependent living.

> "They learn respect for other people's property. Something that somebody else had made has to be respected."

> "They have a responsibility for other kids. Like they may calm down one that's upset . . . they will show sympathy for each other."

Interaction in the classroom was seen as a condition, a setting, in which the qualities of respect and responsibility could be developed and demonstrated. Unlike Orientation D teachers, however, the process of interchange itself was not central in these teachers' thinking. Instead, the requirements for interaction and the outcomes of interaction were highlighted.

Orientation D (40%). Orientation D teachers thought of learning, both personal and cognitive, as highly social in character. Whether talking about group projects, class discussions, or an individual child reading alone or painting at an easel, these teachers perceived that the motivation for the child's work and the meaning of his efforts derived in large part from the social context of the classroom. These teachers therefore made no sharp distinction between independent activities and the social activities that allowed for peer interaction. The classroom itself was perceived in terms of a network of human relationships.

With respect to personal and social growth, teachers of this orientation clearly perceived a reciprocal pattern of influence in what children were learning about themselves and others. They tended to emphasize the sense of self children gain through interaction—a sense of their strengths and weaknesses and of the nature of their interests.

> "One of the important things children learn is how to work together. The teacher is not there to structure everything, and the child has new yardsticks —his own and his peers' opinions. . . . He learns who he is."

> "Children must be part of working out what kind of environment they want to live in. They had to struggle with it and they worked it through. The sooner you get them in touch with each other, the better."

The process of helping one another, of coming to group decisions, of sharing in responsibilities was viewed as engendering an attitude of competence and initiative. This perception was particularly evident in several examples the teachers gave of children undertaking a collective effort to resolve some problem or to improve some aspect of the classroom or school. Such efforts ranged from improving the room arrangement to drawing up suggestions for the principal regarding the daily schedule.

> "They decide what trips to go on, what books to read at meetings, what materials we need. Some of the trips require money, big money for these kids—like when we went ice-skating and to Radio City. But the kids took the initiative for raising money so everyone could go."

> "The attitude encouraged by children learning from each other, making choices, and so on is the process of becoming a self-competent adult."

The teachers also saw in reciprocity a major resource for children's intellectual growth and development. A number of them pointed out the significance of the stimulating effect children have upon one another. The sense of participating in learning with others who have a variety of viewpoints and capabilities was seen as giving a vitality to learning that would be lacking if the same activities were structured on an individualized basis.

"They work better together because they get a better social contact with each other. They respect each other more, and they help each other more . . . plus they stimulate each other more, and this leads to more interesting work whatever they do. I'm thinking of their work with the rods. They get so stimulated that they go much further with concepts than you'd expect of kids of this age. . . .It's just more interesting work."

"Look at all the things you learn from peers as you're growing up. Like all those complicated rules for games. No one stands in front of the classroom and lectures you on it. You learn it because you want to learn it, but no one is pressuring you to learn it right away. If you don't know 'three strikes and you're out,' you can't play; so you learn. Working in groups, a kid is there because he wants to be there."

In conveying their conceptions, some teachers articulated a distinction between interaction in terms of skill exchange (teaching each other) and interaction that stimulated mutual cognitive accommodation. The teacher portrayed in Vignette 2 (Chapter 4) made such a distinction.

"They talk to each other a lot. When they do that, they're defining and redefining their own thoughts as well as what other people say; and that tends to make them more articulate. The other thing I see is that they learn from each other. You know, you couldn't run a class without that. They really *are* the teachers many times."

It is interesting to note that competition, which might be regarded as one way of generating peer interaction, was never mentioned by either this group or by teachers of Orientation C. They did see children stimulating each other, but not in the sense of "outdoing" one another. ("They don't have to kill themselves for my attention.") The extended excerpt below, from an interview, touches on the topic of competition, as it does on many of the points raised about the thinking of teachers in Orientation D.

"It's terrific for the kid who's the helper. It gives him a tremendous amount of self-confidence. And it reinforces various skills that he has or is shaky in. It is very nice also, I think, for children that, instead of the adult always being the one who's giving them information, leading them on, helping them, it's often a child. It is very nice for them to have somebody else who is their size working with them. It's a very equal kind of thing. And

109

even though I don't feel that I'm like this big teacher to them, I still think that it's very nice for the children to be working with each other—period! Do you know what I mean? It's very important to me that the kids work with each other—and the feelings they develop for one another and for other children. I think a lot of that comes from working with each other. Also, they're not afraid. Not that they're afraid with me, but . . . oh, I'm off the track. I think I should drop this because my mind isn't clear at the moment. But I think it is nice for them to be nice to each other. I think that in the old—I shouldn't say this—but in the old system where the teacher would stand at the front of the room and make a competitive thing out of who did their work right and who didn't do their work right, the teacher was unwittingly setting the children against each other, it seems to me. Although we certainly have our friction in the room and we have our arguments and we have a lot of the same things that go on in any classroom, there's still a feeling that develops among the children that's very nice. People come into the room and they comment about the feeling in the room."

"Why did you start to say you shouldn't say this?"

"Well, I don't want to say the 'traditional versus the open classroom' kind of thing and make these broad statements or sweeping judgments."

"But in your observation and from your own experience, you think that in the traditional setting maybe the teacher was perhaps inadvertently fostering a competitive kind of thing?"

"I think so."

"That's interesting. . . . Do you think that children tend to express their needs and feelings more freely in a more open kind of setting?"

"Unquestionably! There's time for it and the teacher is there and can take an interest in what's happening. I was observing—I did this for the first time in a long time this afternoon—I was just observing what was going on in the room and writing it down for myself on a kind of overall basis. And as I was writing, I was thinking to myself—'My God, if I had done this years ago, if I wasn't working in front of the room with the class or giving an assignment for them to do, the class would have fallen apart!' But the room was just functioning beautifully. . . ."

This excerpt was chosen to conclude the section as a way of showing that a teacher's beliefs were not necessarily expressed in a particularly articulate or concise fashion, but in recurring, thematic remarks and in statements of conviction: "working with each other—period!"

* * *

The conceptions of children that teachers hold are pedagogical in nature, fusing a view of learning and development with a view of instruction. The teacher observes and learns about children from a vantage point that is necessarily distinct from those of the parent, the pediatrician, the testmaker, or the research psychologist. Inherent in each of these points of view are constraints and responsibilities that affect how children are perceived and that shape ideas about learning and development. For this reason, we have attempted to organize the coding schemes of this chapter with reference to the educator's viewpoint and did not attempt to portray teachers' perceptions in terms of their resemblance to conceptions within psychology. Thus, the analyses center around constructs about children as learners in the classroom.

CHAPTER
6
PHENOMENOLOGICAL INQUIRY

In our initial study of open education, child-as-resource constructs were identified as pivotal in differentiating an interactive view of education from other child-centered positions and from prescribed curriculum-centered positions.

> In contrast to those educational theories which *assume* the presence of a child during instruction, [this] approach *requires* the presence of a child to define instruction. (Bussis and Chittenden, 1970, p. 15)

The emphasis on child-as-resource also clearly contrasts with the idea of child-as-deficient, an idea that underlies many diagnostic and remedial programs.

Throughout the previous chapter, conceptions of the child-as-resource for learning and instruction have constituted a framework for organizing the teachers' views. Thus, Orientation A represents a view of children as almost devoid of resources or qualities significant for teaching. Orientations B and C represent variations in both the kinds of qualities that teachers perceive in children and in the extent to which these qualities are seen as relevant for teaching and learning. Orientation D represents a view of these qualities as integral to instruction and learning. In summary, Orientations A through D approximate gradations in conviction and consistency of the central construct of child-as-resource.

Just as a particular understanding of the potential value of materials is related to a teacher's ability to "see connections" between surface curriculum and organizing curricular priorities, so phenomenological inquiry is related to perceiving the child-as-resource. The present chapter examines the significance of phenomenological inquiry in the teachers' analyses of children's learning. Specifically, it considers the importance of observing and inquiring as explicit strategies in teaching. More generally, it considers the nature of observations that teachers reported in responding to questions throughout the curriculum/child portion of the interview.

"Phenomenological inquiry" is inquiry directed to trying to understand another person's viewpoint. It should be noted at the outset that such inquiry may take the form of questioning, or it may take the form of reflective observation in which no direct interchange occurs. In either case, the purpose of the inquiry is to gain a better understanding of the other person's meanings, interpretations, and ways of construing a situation. Thus, phenomenological inquiry is very different in nature from various forms of diagnostic inquiry that are used for the purpose of placing a person on a scale or in a category system that is external to the individual's perspective.

People do not necessarily inquire phenomenologically in carrying out the transactions of everyday life. On observing that someone characteristically acts in an impulsive fashion, we may use the information for deciding how best to interact with him, but we need not concern ourselves with finding out whether he views his behavior as impulsive or not. Even when we do inquire why a person did something, it is often for the purpose of obtaining a reason we consider rational rather than for the purpose of gaining some insight into his viewpoint. "Why did you do that?" is frequently a request for an explanation that will satisfy the questioner.

When teachers guide children's learning, they assume a special kind of leadership. Within the terms of construct theory, assuming a role of leadership *requires* the capacity for phenomenological inquiry. As is clear in the following quotation from Kelly (1955a) however, to attempt to understand the child's viewpoint does not mean that the inquirer must think like a child.

> . . . the person who is to play a constructive role in a social process with another person need not so much construe things as the other person does as he must effectively construe the other person's outlook. (p. 95)

The teacher's responsibility for considering the child's view has been emphasized by some writers. Frances Hawkins (1969), for example, in an account of her teaching says, "I prefer to be told little, to be forced to observe much" (p. 9). This does not mean that she rejects the validity of other people's appraisals of children (as she explains at a later point), but rather refers to the danger of looking at children in preemptive ways and thus missing much by not really observing for oneself. Jones (1968) is rather adamant about the central place of the child's phenomenological world in teaching.

> I submit that the prime media of this art [of teaching] are no less than the subjective uncertainties, the subjective risks, and the subjective goals which the children can be expected to bring in bewilderingly individual ways to any good curriculum. . . . (p. 113)

Data that bear on the place of phenomenological inquiry in the teachers' analyses of learning and instruction were derived from two sources. The first was discussions of inquiry per se and/or observations of children in which inquiry was clearly an intentional strategy. The second, more tangential, analysis was derived through coding teachers' anecdotes and observations for evidence of permeability of child constructs—i.e., evidence that constructs could incorporate new and unanticipated information about children.

INQUIRY AS AN EXPLICIT STRATEGY

Some teachers in the study discussed and emphasized the process of inquiry (either observation or questioning) in its own right as important to teaching.

> "During the afternoon I do activities with the kids and I observe a lot [because] I'm trying to get a closer correlation between the morning and afternoon. I also observe how they are interacting socially without an adult around."

> "I'd like to learn how to observe children better. I don't think people understand how important it is to observe . . . my advisor's great at it. . . . If you can see how children are doing things, you can take them a step further."

"There are so many ways of finding out . . . I might ask a question. For instance, a child said 'Columbus discovered America.' Well, what does that mean—what does 'discovering America' mean? This child didn't really know. Now on a formal test he would have 'known.' We had a whole discussion about what discovering something meant. There are so many other examples. A child asked what moving from one month to another means. You know, 'What happens after March 31?' [pause] I think the longer you work with children the more you pick up questions like that. For example, all the children were bringing up 'Stop the war in Vietnam.' Well, they don't know what Vietnam is, and they don't really have an understanding of war. So we tried to talk about war and related it to specific situations that the children were involved in. Like punching someone when he has just touched you, or pushing. The children brought up what peace is. Peace might be 'talking things over' or 'helping someone.' The same with brotherhood— a very hard concept for a first-grade child to understand. These things are always thrown at them by adults, and they just pick up on saying clichés they know are 'right' but don't really understand."

Other teachers indicated an awareness of the importance of observation, but they found it difficult and seemed to equate inquiry with a direct interrogation of the child rather than with a more flexible "discussion" of the kind noted above.

"When I ask them what they're interested in, they usually say they don't know. You learn a lot more from observing . . . but it's hard."

For the most part, however, evidence for coding phenomenological inquiry did not come from explicit discussions of the processes of observing and asking questions, but from concrete examples in which inquiry played an implicit though obvious role. In the following example the comments focus on children's learning, but the significance of observation is evident.

"I've watched them. Right now they have gotten into mixing colors. There have been three five-year-olds there just discussing the process of making colors . . . 'If I put blue and yellow together, what color is that going to make?' . . . They are really experimenting with it. They take a paper and they do this, and at the end of the day they have a picture that's just one big blob. You wouldn't know what it was—unless you saw the process."

116

For purposes of coding, two areas were included: (1) evidence of inquiry into, or clear acknowledgement of, the child's understandings and cognitive perspective; and (2) evidence of inquiry into the child's feelings. Mere acknowledgment of feelings was not considered strong enough evidence to be given credit for a phenomenological approach to children. As in most of the illustrations above, inquiry referred to attempts to consider or to find out about the child's view of things. It did not refer to attempts to diagnose skill deficiencies according to some external checklist—although one teacher with several instances of inquiry remarked: "You can even observe minute things, like whether a child knows the *sh* sound or not."

Twenty-five teachers (42% of the sample) were coded for clear evidence of inquiry into the child's perspective. Not surprisingly, these 25 were not distributed randomly across all the orientations, A through D, with respect to children's (1) needs and feelings, (2) interests and choice, and (3) social interaction. There was a strong relationship between teachers who construed resources for instruction and learning in all or in some of these qualities (Orientation D) and evidence of phenomenological inquiry. Table 13 indicates the extent of this relationship.

Table 13

Relationship Between Evidence of Phenomenological Inquiry and
Teachers' Perceptions of Children's Needs and Feelings,
Interests and Choice, and Social Interaction

Pattern of Orientations (A-D) for the Three Types of Qualities Perceived in Children	Total Sample		Number and Percentage of Teachers Coded for Phenomenological Inquiry Within Each Pattern	
	N	%	N	%
Consistent D Orientation	12	20	10	83
One or Two D Orientations (no A)	17	28	12	71
Combinations of B & C Orientations	11	18	2	18
One or Two A Orientations (no D)	14	23	1	7
Consistent A Orientation	6	10	0	-
	60		25	

As can be seen from Table 13, of the 20 teachers who were coded for one or two A orientations or who had a consistent pattern of A orientation, only one gave any clear evidence of phenomenological inquiry. Whether this lack of inquiry stems from their perceptions that children's qualities do not offer much for instruction, or whether their perceptions of children's qualities suffer from lack of inquiry, seem moot questions. The point illustrated in Table 13 is that teachers who tended to perceive the child-as-resource for learning and instruction (consistent or partial D orientation) also tended to inquire into the child's perspective—and apparently found such inquiry an invaluable aid in their teaching. In fact, these teachers seemed to assume that phenomenological inquiry was a *necessary condition* for successful teaching in an open classroom.

PERMEABILITY OF CHILD CONSTRUCTS

Many teachers who did not give evidence of active inquiry into the child's perspective nonetheless showed signs of permeability in their thinking about children. A construct system is permeable to the extent that observations of children are not directed or filtered by preconceived ideas about child behavior. A permeable construct system is open to dissonant or surprising information, and it is marked by a "freshness" of observation. In coding, evidence of permeability was judged by comments that had a ring of child-realism to them, comments in which the children came through as individuals and in which the teacher may have noted unexpected aspects of children's behavior. Accounts that were strewn with slogans and stereotypic labelings of children were considered the opposite of permeability. The most obvious examples of labeling are found in such statements as: "Low IQ children have trouble with choice"; "Manipulative materials are good for the immature ones because they like to be active"; "My sixes need more reassurance than my sevens"; "The disruptive ones have short attention spans."

It is interesting to note that permeability may be quite independent of a teacher's particular views about learning and instruction. Thus, teachers who were coded for permeability (freshness) in observation did not necessarily connect these observations of children with any thoughts about the teaching and learning process. Observations could be duly noted, but apparently not used. The first excerpt below illustrates a "fresh" observation in which there is only the slightest hint of a connection with learning or development. The second excerpt illustrates a "fresh" observation that led no further than the making of it.

118

"The animals give them an opportunity to express affection. The most active kid when you give him an animal will just sit and cuddle that animal. A lot of children, I think, don't have a chance to be soft with something. The animal doesn't tell them what to do . . . it's that sort of thing."

"The things they talk about they really want. One little boy is constantly talking about fish, and it turns out he wants to be a marine biologist. The children don't laugh at one another in discussion; they're really serious. One little girl said she wished she could be a nurse so she could look at men in bed. They really say what they mean!"

Ratings of permeability, based on the entire curriculum/child portion of the interview, were made on a four-point scale, as follows:

Rating 3—"Freshness" of observation is thematic; it occurs in several contexts of the interview.

Rating 2—"Freshness" of observation is obvious but not pervasive. There are two or three clear instances in the interview.

Rating 1—Limited or weak evidence of "freshness" in the interview.

Rating 0—No evidence of "freshness."

The relationship between this coding and the pattern of teachers' orientations toward children's resources is presented in Table 14. The trend in these data is similar to that shown in Table 13. Teachers who perceive more significant qualities in children also tend to describe more vivid and realistic observations about children. More interesting, however, is the fact that 48 teachers (80% of the sample) were coded as showing *some* evidence of permeability or freshness in their observations. This is almost twice the number of those who were coded as exhibiting evidence of phenomenological inquiry.

The fact that a great many teachers in the sample were "seeing children" in nonstereotypic ways is reminiscent of the finding discussed at the beginning of Chapter 5. There we remarked that virtually all of the teachers said they "knew more" about children in response to the question: "Do you consider judging individual children's progress to be more, or less, difficult in an informal setting?" It was also pointed out that "knowing the

Table 14

Relationship Between Permeability in Observation and
Teachers' Perceptions of Children's Needs and
Feelings, Interests and Choice, and Social Interaction

Pattern of Orientations (A-D) for the Three Types of Qualities Perceived in Children	N	Distribution of Permeability Ratings (0-3) Within Each Pattern			
		0	1	2	3
Consistent D Orientation	12	—	1	2	9
One or Two D Orientations (no A)	17	—	5	11	1
Combinations of B & C Orientations	11	2	1	6	2
One or Two A Orientations (no D)	14	4	8	1	1
Consistent A Orientation	6	6	—	—	—
	60	12	15	20	13

children better" was frequently mentioned as one of the benefits of teaching in an open classroom. On the basis of data presented in this chapter, we would interpret the many comments about "knowing children better" as meaning that the teachers were being receptive to a broader array of information from children. If this is so, it represents a step in the direction of more perceptive observation. The problem, however, is that nearly half of the teachers who described children with some degree of freshness did not show any evidence of *active* inquiry into the child's perspective. Like the benefit of "knowing children better," richer observations of children were apparently regarded by many teachers as a result or an outcome of teaching informally. Several teachers remarked at some time during the interview that "there's more to see," but while recognizing this phenomenon, they seemed to treat it as a bonus of the open classroom. Unlike teachers who were intentionally inquiring into the child's perspective, they did not seem to consider observation as a necessary condition for teaching informally.

THE TEACHER-AS-INVESTIGATOR

In the folklore about teaching, as in the literature, it is sometimes claimed that teachers cannot see children—because they must teach. This argument asserts that the teacher's vantage point is so enveloped by external criteria that not only does the individual child disappear from view, but the outlook leads to an impoverished conception of children in general. Data presented in this chapter and in the previous one lend some support to this claim. Teachers with a consistent A orientation and some of those with one or two A orientations did present a narrow conception of children's qualities, and they gave few signs of seeing children as persons. They tended to see children in terms of grade-levels, degrees of maturity-immaturity, basal reader progress, IQ categories, and the like. It should be noted that all of the teachers in the study were operating within a context that required attention to grades, tests, and, in some instances, to specific performance objectives. These external criteria for evaluation inevitably must pull in a direction that detracts from a phenomenological approach calling for observation and evaluative judgment that is responsive to a particular child in a particular context.

On the other hand, it has also been asserted that teachers—again, because they teach—are potentially capable of studying human development and learning in greater depth and richness than is possible in most research investigations. David Hawkins points out that the prolonged and continuous interactions in a classroom and school have a reality that laboratory studies and most field studies cannot attain. In particular, when teachers have created a setting that engages the capabilities of children, they are in a position to devise formulations about learning and teaching that are far more comprehensive than the formulations that characterize most evaluation instruments and that underlie much of educational research. As a case in point, the integrated child-as-resource constructs of many teachers in this study would not be accommodated by typical evaluation designs that assess educational programs through measures that separate how a child feels about learning (affective measures) from what he learns (achievement measures).

Data from the interview study also lend support to Hawkins' ideas about teaching and research. Although few teachers in the study conceived of teaching as a research investigation, many clearly saw it as an investigative process. Those combining a sharpness of observation and inquiry, as described in this chapter, with integrated conceptions of learning, as described in the previous chapter, are looking at children in ways that should be challenging to research. For these teachers, the so-called "gap between theory and practice" is not the type of gap usually

121

implied by that phrase. As Hawkins (1966) states with reference to psychology and the study of learning: "Our efforts are being made, I believe, in an historical situation where the best practice excels the best theory in quite essential ways; this fact defines a strategy we ought to follow" (p. 3). Along with Hawkins, we believe that the integration of research and practice can perhaps only come about when practice is a more integral part of research. The observing and inquiring teacher is an invaluable and virtually untapped source for the development of insightful theory.

THE WORKING ENVIRONMENT OF THE SCHOOL

This chapter and the next discuss the teachers' responses to the second portion of the interview, the *working environment* section. Thus, they address questions of in-service development and of conditions that foster and support such development.

In conducting the last part of the interview, we placed major emphasis upon the teachers' perceptions of the advisory program. Although the role of an external advisory program was most prominent in our thinking at the time, we were also concerned with institutional resources that characterized the schools in which the teachers worked—resources such as other teachers, aides and paraprofessionals, parents, the principal, institutional policies and procedures. It is these resources for development within the school that constitute the subject of this chapter. Perceptions of support from external advisors are analyzed in Chapter 8.

THE NATURE OF ADULT RELATIONSHIPS

The manner in which adults interact with one another has a direct bearing on the educational environment that is created for children and adults alike. The pattern of relationships among adults within a school is extremely complex, however, especially in schools undertaking change. Since questions regarding adult interaction were raised at the end of the interview and were not pursued in great detail, our discussion only touches on the many issues involved and is limited to but a few aspects of the teachers' perceptions.

OTHER TEACHERS

The teachers in this study were not experimenting with team teaching in the sense of formally dividing instructional responsibilities for a given group of children. The programs in which they participated, however, were trying to promote greater teacher interaction on matters ranging from constructive criticism to the sharing of materials. The intent was to foster a climate of professional dialogue and support. The purpose of promoting a learning community among teachers is perhaps most explicitly discussed in the literature of the Open Corridor program, although it is central to the other programs as well.

> Real underpinnings for growth and development come from the communal feeling existing between teachers. . . . The exchange of ideas, sharing of materials and teaching techniques, and evaluation of curricula enable teachers to assist each other in their new understanding of how children learn. (Hazlewood and Norris, 1971, p. 11)

In the interview, the teachers were asked to describe the nature and extent of cooperative work with other teachers in the school and to comment on the perceived benefits and/or disadvantages of such cooperation. Before characterizing some differences in the responses to these questions, it should be noted that over 90% of the sample perceived that there was at present more cooperative interaction among the teachers than had previously been the case, and that this change was for the better.

Nevertheless, many teachers (33%) described themselves as working, for the most part, independently of other teachers in the school, with the exception of field trips, staff meetings, and workshop gatherings. They were not necessarily satisfied with this situation, however, since many looked forward to more extensive interaction.

A little over half of the sample (54%) viewed their interaction with other teachers as a very significant part of their teaching. Interactions occurred over lunch, via phone calls in the evening, in after-school meetings or workshops, and in informal exchanges in the hallways. These interactions were perceived either as dealing with "practical matters," such as ideas about materials or new activities, or as relating to emotional support. ("Without her encouragement in that first year, I never would have made it!") As a group, these teachers were alike in the kinds of benefits they ascribed to interaction, but they differed noticeably in the extent to which they actually joined other teachers or included other children in the course of their daily functioning. Thus, for 13 teachers in this group there was relatively little evidence of exchange of children. For the remaining 18, however, the participation of children from other grades and classrooms was a common occurrence, and the participation of other teachers in the classroom was an occasional occurrence. Such participation was sometimes formally planned; at other times it occurred on the spur of the moment.

Finally, a small group of teachers (12%) perceived their interaction as including the elements noted above and as extending to the level of constructive criticism. In their accounts, talking with other teachers was an important stimulus to the reformulation of their own analyses of where they were headed as teachers. They perceived a reciprocity in the relationship that was vital to the development of their capabilities to evaluate and examine what went on in their classroom and school.

In summary, then, the picture that emerges from the teachers' accounts is one of moving away from isolation of the kind depicted by McPherson (1972). The teachers welcomed the climate of a freer interchange among adults, as they had welcomed the freer interchange among children. But at the time of the interview, this interchange was portrayed as centering more upon the practical and emotional immediacy of teaching than upon the analysis and examination of basic curricular and instructional issues.

The following excerpts convey the flavor of these various perceptions.

"Great feeling of community which public schools never had before."

"We have skills to share. One teacher might be good at room arrangement and can share this ability with other teachers."

"If you are isolated from other adults, you feel locked in to the world of children and lose perspective."

"Friendly relations between teachers are good for children to see."

"[The benefits of interaction are] sharing ideas, seeing another person work, seeing that other people have problems, getting to know teachers as human beings. If you have a sense of community, the problem for one teacher would be a problem for all teachers. This helps teachers to grow . . . and it helps children."

AIDES

Forty-five of the teachers in the sample had the assistance of an aide or paraprofessional in their classrooms for half of the day or more. (In New York City the term *paraprofessional* is used; at other sites *aide* is the common designation. The term *aide* will be used throughout for the sake of brevity, but with the understood connotation of professional development that is associated with the term *paraprofessional.*) At all sites, local or federal guidelines stipulated that the position of aide be accessible to members of the community without college degrees or teaching certificates. It was often seen as a position of opportunity for development toward becoming a teacher. These guidelines meant that the teacher and aide differed in educational background and that often the aide was a parent from the community.

Three kinds of questions were raised with teachers concerning the aides. These questions sought the teachers' views on the contributions the aide made, the satisfactions that the aide derived from the position, and the major differences (if any) between the role of designated teacher and the role of the aide.

Teachers' accounts of the aides' duties and responsibilities revealed a range of perceptions, from ones in which the aide was completely subordinate to the teacher and undertook menial tasks with little responsibility, to a relationship that was perceived as that of a colleague. Seven teachers (15%) described the aides' work as being consistently subordinate and as calling for limited exercise of judgment. Correcting workbooks, keeping house, and taking children to the cafeteria were typical examples. For the most part, there was little evidence that these teachers perceived that more could or would be expected of the aide. One teacher remarked that an aide "can take over unless the teacher is careful that she does what is an aide's job." Seventeen teachers (38%) described the aide as responsible for carrying out many activities that were essentially identical to the teacher's. Thus, the aide conducted reading groups, participated in mathematics projects, assisted children in writing stories, and worked along with the teacher in attending to routine matters. Although the

126

activities were similar to those of the teacher, these teachers emphasized that the aide had to be trained or supervised fairly closely.

In the perceptions of a third group of 16 teachers (35%), the aide was again seen as carrying out many of the responsibilities and activities of the teacher, but there was definitely a greater expectation that the aide was capable and would take initiative in a variety of ways. ("She's been excellent in gaining the interests of some of the poorer readers.") Special interests or talents were often noted, and ways sought to relate them to the life of the classroom. ("Her abilities in music offset my inabilities.") These teachers did, however, retain responsibility for overall planning and coordination of the day's activities.

Finally, a small group of five teachers (11%) perceived little significant difference between their role in the classroom and that of the aide. Both shared the responsibility for all kinds of instructional matters, ranging from planning to classroom management. ("She's really just another teacher.") Nonetheless, teachers in this group perceived themselves as instrumental in setting the tone of the classroom, and they felt that accountability to parents and administration, as well as legal responsibility, resided with them. In daily functioning, however, they saw little difference. ("She [the aide] gets paid about one-third of what I get, for doing the same things.")

In conclusion, for the majority of teachers the experience of having another adult as an intimate part of the classroom was a relatively new one. For many, this was only the second year of working with an aide. They all stressed the value of such assistance, and many seemed very much aware of the complexity of the relationship and of the need to work toward establishing a productive interaction.

> "It's complicated. For one thing, how do I 'supervise' somebody who is so much older and has gone through so much more than I have . . . yet isn't aware of many things the children need to learn?"

> "This year I don't feel my aide really believes in it. She still believes there should be more set things kids have to do. . . . Her influence has pulled me back. You would think that the teacher has to be the strong one, but I'm very influenced by who I'm working with."

> "I think the whole teacher-aide relationship is a very tricky, delicate, very subtle one. It's a problem of balance.

For both teacher and aide to get satisfaction, a lot of things have to be functioning well. Satisfaction comes from two people liking each other, doing something they like, and working together. It's important for children to see two adults working out a relationship—much in the same way we want children to work out a relationship."

PARENTS

At the time of the interview, the question of parent involvement in schools was very much a part of public discussions about the changing nature of schools as institutions. In New York City, the move toward decentralization brought with it cause for considerable reexamination of the teacher/parent relationship. In a few schools, the parents—more so than some of the teachers that were interviewed—had been instrumental in establishing an open education program. The original Follow Through guidelines had called for community involvement in the selection of a program sponsor, and attention to the role of parents constituted an important aspect of the implementation of the program. In a 1972 restatement of their position, EDC stressed the significance of parents:

> With the help of teachers, aides, local advisors, and EDC advisors, the administration should make an on-going effort to help parents understand the open education program and the learning experiences their children are having. The administration should also make a determined effort to provide opportunities for parents to help Follow Through staff to understand the children, the community, the life style of those being served. Parents must be always welcomed in the school and encouraged to participate and observe in classrooms; there must also be established some mechanism through which parents can receive prompt and sympathetic consideration of their grievances. (p. 5)

Two sets of questions in the interview centered on the topic of parents. The first inquired about parent participation in the classroom and other forms of parent contribution and influence. The second took up the matter of how well parents understood the teachers' goals—or the goals of the program.

On the topic of parent participation, most of the teachers (75%) asserted that parents were welcome to visit the classroom and to join some of the activities. However, with probing, it was apparent that the percentage of classrooms in which a fair

128

number of parents actually worked was considerably smaller. One form of participation was the utilization of special skills and interests. Cooking, sewing, carpentry, photography, and knowledge of animals were examples offered. Six teachers (11%) did not welcome parents except for scheduled conferences, and the remainder (13%) extended invitations for informal visits only on special occasions, such as a classroom puppet show or a holiday party.

Concerning the parents' understandings of the goals of the programs, the teachers were uncertain about a number of things. Some stated at the outset that "I really don't know what the parents think" despite a good deal of contact. Several talked of subgroups among the parents, some understanding and supporting the program and others fighting it. There were also parents who were supportive but apparently without understanding.

"Very often they approve of what's going on, but don't really understand what you're doing. The old notions of what a school is will take a long time to die."

The impression gained from this section of the interview is that teachers were very much in flux in the development of their ideas about home and school relationships. They seemed for the most part to feel strongly that parents should have a more significant place in the school, but were uncertain about the implications for the teacher's responsibilities and did not know how to commence. On the question of understanding goals, the uncertainty was compounded by the teacher's own changing understandings of goals.

"It's hard to explain to parents when your own accomplishment of goals varies, and you have goals of different kinds. It's easy to explain reading goals, but I need to do a better job with my high priority, broader goals."

RATINGS OF TEACHERS' PERCEPTIONS

In addition to categorizing the content of responses to the working environment section of the interview, teachers' remarks were also rated for several general qualities. The two ratings of concern are: (1) complexity of views about other adult roles and institutional policies, and (2) initiative in the development of working relationships. A global five-point scale was used to indicate amount of evidence for these qualities in the teachers' responses to questions concerning other teachers, aides, parents, the principal, and the school as an institution.

129

Perceived Complexity of Roles. This was a rating of evidence that the teacher perceived the different functions of a role (e.g., that a principal dealt with district policies, with parent groups, with fiscal problems) or that a particular function was seen as consisting of differentiated elements (e.g., that a principal's relationship to parents could call for responsiveness to parents' negative perceptions of teachers and at the same time maintain support for teachers).

Development of Working Relationships. This rating was intended to reflect the extent to which the teacher apparently took the initiative in utilizing and developing the resources represented by other adults or in changing institutional policies that hampered child or adult functioning. Thus, identifying the interests or capabilities of parents and bringing about their connection to the school or classroom would be grounds for a high rating with respect to parents. Similarly, efforts to initiate changes in school policies would be evidence for a high rating with respect to the school. A high rating was based on reports of actions that the teacher had taken, or that it seemed reasonably safe to infer had been taken. In other words, ideas about promoting adult resources that had never been translated into action were insufficient evidence for a high rating.

Percentage distributions of the ratings shown in Table 15 suggest several general points. First, at every site the aides and parents were clearly salient in the teachers' thinking, as indicated by their comparatively high ratings on both scales. As mentioned previously, the roles of aides and parents, as defined by the open education programs, represented relatively new roles for many teachers. The newness, coupled with the omnipresent quality of another adult in the classroom, undoubtedly contributed to the salience.

The data on the development of working relationships also suggest that there was comparatively little evidence of teacher initiative and effort to change or develop school policies. The school and the principal were perceived somewhat more as "givens" of the teaching situation, and unlike aides, parents, and, to some extent, other teachers, the teachers seemed less inclined to make moves toward modifying the status quo. Regulations and policies of the school were often complained about, but equally often were accepted as inevitable and unchangeable. A "chaotic" lunch situation was one frequently mentioned example. The interference of custodial policies was another recurring topic (e.g., rugs not allowed because there were no vacuum cleaners), although there were many more signs here of teacher initiative in

Table 15
Ratings of Teachers' Perceptions of the Working Environment

Perceived Complexity of Roles in the Working Environment

	Much Evidence 5	4	Some Evidence 3	2	No Evidence 1	N[1]	Mean
Aides	13%	27%	40%	18%	2%	45	3.3
Parents	9	33	36	22	0	58	3.3
Other Teachers	5	19	37	28	11	57	2.8
Principal	4	20	29	36	13	55	2.7
School	9	25	27	31	7	55	3.0

Initiative in the Development of Working Relationships

	Much Evidence 5	4	Some Evidence 3	2	No Evidence 1	N[1]	Mean
Aides	16%	28%	21%	23%	12%	43	3.1
Parents	14	40	22	19	5	58	3.4
Other Teachers	3	21	29	36	10	58	2.7
Principal	4	7	22	34	33	55	2.1
School	2	12	34	25	27	56	2.4

[1]The variation of N arises from the fact that 15 teachers had no aide and, in certain instances, because of time pressures to complete the interview, a section of the working environment portion was omitted or raised so briefly that it did not warrant a rating.

alleviating problems and in negotiating changes with custodial staff. Questions about the principal elicited extremely varied reactions among the teachers. This was true even of teachers within a single school. Thus, one person might hold a very favorable view of the principal ("he's tremendously supportive"), and another person a negative view of the same individual ("he's a tour guide"). Regardless of the viewpoint expressed, however, few teachers talked about actions to improve a poor working relationship with the principal or about efforts to make a good working relationship better.

131

Ratings for development of a working relationship with other teachers fall somewhere between the higher ratings for aides and parents and the lower ones for administration and school. Working with colleagues was extremely important to almost all of the teachers, but there was less evidence of steps taken to strengthen or modify such relationships than was true for aides and parents. If a group of teachers functioned well together, it was apt to be ascribed to the good fortune of finding oneself among "congenial people" and not to planning or otherwise working toward such functioning. Although there were, of course, many exceptions to this general point, the ratings nonetheless reflect the fact that the teachers also tended to accept other teachers as "givens" of the situation.

We have a general impression, difficult to document further, that teachers can hold differentiated views about those who are most immediately affected by their teaching—the children, the aide, the parents—and yet be vaguer and perhaps less informed about institutional and administrative policies.

ADULT-AS-RESOURCE AND CHILD-AS-RESOURCE

As illustrated in some of the remarks quoted earlier in this chapter, a number of teachers were explicit in pointing out the connection between the ways in which adults relate to one another and the kind of educational setting created for children. Mutual assistance, sharing, exchange of ideas, and working to improve a relationship were qualities that these teachers wanted in their schools as well as in their classrooms.

In order to examine more closely the relationship between teachers' beliefs about working with adults and their beliefs about children, a comparison was made between ratings on development of working relationships and the summary of teachers' orientations toward child-as-resource as presented in Chapter 6. The *global ratings* (derived from the working environment portion of the interview) are similar to the *orientations* (derived from the curriculum/child portion) to the extent that both codings reflect the identification of potential learning qualities in persons or in situations. Seen in this light, an orientation toward adult-as-resource may be part of the same teaching construct system as an orientation toward child-as-resource.

The data in Table 16 show the relationship between the ratings of working with adults and the codings of child-as-resource. For a number of teachers at least, these data suggest a psychological consistency in thinking about adults and children. Thus, to examine the extremes, three of the six teachers with consistent A orientations (who saw no resources in children) also had low mean ratings on development of working relationships with adults, and the other three had moderate ratings. At the other extreme, of the twelve teachers given consistent D orientations (who saw high resources in children), eight were given a high mean rating for developing adult resources.

Table 16

Relationship Between Views Toward Child-as-Resource and
Views Toward Adult-as-Resource

Range of Mean[1] Ratings: Development of Working Relationships	Pattern of Orientations (A-D) for Qualities Perceived in Children's Needs and Feelings, Interests and Choice, and Social Interaction[2]					
	D only	D partial	C/B only	A partial	A only	Total[3]
	N	N	N	N	N	
1.0 - 2.5 (low)	2	5	5	3	3	18
2.6 - 3.5 (middle)	2	6	4	7	3	22
3.6 - 5.0 (high)	8	6	2	2	0	18

[1]Mean based on ratings for relationships with other teachers, parents, and with aides (where applicable).

[2]See tables in Chapters 5 and 6 for explication of patterns of orientation.

[3]Incomplete working environment data for two teachers account for an N of 58.

In some ways, the teachers who do not fit the pattern are as interesting as those who do. As the table indicates, there were four teachers who appeared to have been very active in working toward more satisfactory relationships with parents, other teachers, and aides (a high rating), but who did not perceive children in as rich a manner (Orientations C/B only or A partial). For example, one teacher with a high adult-as-resource rating had worked diligently to become a part of the open education program, was very active in parent/teacher affairs, and encouraged a great deal of participation on the part of the aide; yet, the coding of orientation toward children indicated that, throughout her efforts to "individualize" instruction, she

133

maintained a conception of children's learning as being essentially receptive and noninteractive. Another teacher was articulate about her activities in working for change within the school and community but much vaguer and undifferentiated in her thinking about children.

Representing a different type of exception to the general pattern were those teachers with articulated views of children's resources (consistent D orientation), but who generally perceived that there was little to work with in the adult environment of the school. For example, two teachers clearly saw potential in the child (D only) but were resentful toward the principal, suspicious of parent pressure, and isolated from most of the staff (low adult-as-resource rating). They taught behind closed doors. It is interesting to note that these teachers and two others, with relatively high child codings but middle or low adult ratings, were all teaching in schools with no advisory and with no clear commitment to an open education program. One of these teachers reported that, during her first tentative efforts to have children work together and help each other, the principal declared: "Well, if children really could teach each other, we wouldn't need teachers, would we?"

Despite the influence of a particular school setting in bringing about a discrepancy between views toward children and toward adults, the data in Table 16 generally point up the fact that construct systems regarding the development of human resources can embrace beliefs about children and about adults. Evidence of this kind of integration of constructs is supportive for the rationale of this study. In this respect, it should be emphasized that the data in Table 16 are based on codings from two major sections of the interview, one focusing on children and the other on adults, and that there was an interval of many months between the codings of the two sections.

The working environment ratings reflect how the teachers construed the situations in which they worked and, thus, are quite different from the usual situational or status variables that are studied in much research. Tables 17 and 18 report data on the relationship between child-as-resource orientations and two variables of the latter type—grade level of current teaching position and years of teaching experience. Table 17 indicates that grade level is not associated with orientation toward children in any consistent manner. In this regard, it is interesting to note that the kindergarten teachers do not differ from the primary grade teachers in child orientation codings—this despite the tradition of the greater child centeredness of kindergarten. Although the

Table 17

Grade Level of Teaching Position and Views Toward Child-as-Resource

Grade Level(s)[1]	Pattern of Orientations (A-D) for Perceptions of Children's Needs and Feelings, Interests and Choice, and Social Interaction					Total
	D only	D partial	C/B only	A partial	A only	
	N	N	N	N	N	
Kindergarten	2	2	1	5	0	10
First	3	5	4	4	3	19
Second	2	5	3	2	3	15
Third & higher	5	5	3	3	0	16

[1]Thirteen teachers taught a combination of two grade levels. These were grouped according to the higher of the two grade levels.

surface curriculum for these kindergarten teachers as a group reflected this traditional child focus, the child-as-resource codings in Table 17 revealed a variety of basic perceptions of children comparable to the variety perceived by teachers at other grade levels.

Table 18 shows that the number of teachers with views toward children that are generally more congruent with open education (Orientations D only and D partial) was highest in the least experienced group. In interpreting this result, it should be stressed that, in the present study, all teachers with two years of experience (and half of those with three years) had never worked in a teaching situation other than the open education program in which they were participating at the time of the interview. In addition, some of them had come from preservice programs in open education. Therefore, the closer match between their orientations and those of the programs is understandable.

Considering the three more experienced groups of teachers, there is little evidence of a relationship between experience and views of the child. Moreover, teachers with similar views of children perceived their past experiences in very different ways. Some teachers with much experience (and high child-as-resource

135

Table 18

Years of Teaching Experience and Views Toward Child-as-Resource

Range of Years of Experience	Pattern of Orientations (A-D) for Perceptions of Children's Needs and Feelings, Interests and Choice, and Social Interaction					Total
	D only	D partial	C/B only	A partial	A only	
	N	N	N	N	N	
2 - 3	7	8	2	1	1	19
4 - 6	2	4	3	4	2	15
7 - 10	1	4	2	6	1	14
11 - 29	2	1	4	3	2	12

codings) perceived continuity in the development of their thinking. They saw the open education program or the school as stimulating and supportive of a general direction in teaching toward which they had always worked. One teacher with 15 years of experience in an approach apparently less conventional than that of her colleagues and administrators saw the advisory as bringing encouragement and reassurance that she was "on the right track." They brought "ideas and sanity." Her past experiences, which included teaching in Head Start, were seen as highly relevant to her current thinking. On the other hand, other equally experienced teachers, holding similar child-as-resource views, saw such an abrupt discontinuity between their past and present approaches that they spontaneously labeled themselves as "beginning" teachers.

> "My first year in the program was like starting all over, despite 12 years. I think I worked harder, made more mistakes, learned more that year than I did in my first years of teaching."

Phenomenologically at least, such teachers could well be placed with the "real" beginning teachers.

CHAPTER

8

TEACHERS' PERCEPTIONS OF SUPPORT FROM ADVISORS

"The advisory grows more proficient each year. They've changed greatly in the three years I've been in the program . . . for the better. They're new at the job too, and I can't think of a harder job. It's like the hardest aspects of teaching. . . ."

In the spring of 1972, when we conducted the interviews, the role of an advisor was one of the newest roles in education. At that time, the two "oldest" programs in the country (the EDC Follow Through program and the CCNY Open Corridor program) had four years of beginning experience, each having been modestly initiated in the 1968-69 school year with only a handful of classrooms and advisors between them. Community Resources Institute began its advising activities in 1970, in seven classrooms and with a staff of two.

At the time of the interview, 154 classrooms were in the EDC program, and its advisory staff had grown to 18. The Open Corridor program, which began with its director as the only advisor, had grown to a staff of 13 advisors who were working with 137 classroom teachers. In short, the role of an advisor was an evolving role in 1972. With the continual entry of new teachers into the programs, with the development of teachers experienced in the programs, and with the gradual expansion of the programs into the middle and upper elementary school grades, the job of an advisor has by no means become a routine and clearly circumscribed set of procedures. On the contrary, the job of advising becomes increasingly complex, especially as the range of experience widens among advisors themselves, and calls for increasingly comprehensive strategies of support and development for teachers and advisors alike. It is still an evolving role. This point, though not essential to understanding the findings discussed in this chapter, is essential for interpreting the discussion in an appropriate context.

The most general finding regarding teachers' perceptions of support from advisors comes from a question at the end of the interview which asked for a summary evaluation of the working environment.

> Thinking back over all the people and resources that we have been talking about (the advisory, parents, aides, other teachers, principal)—what or who do you consider have been major sources of help and support in accomplishing your teaching objectives?

Each source of support mentioned by a teacher was rated on a three-point scale as follows: (1) mentioned in passing, or mentioned as a help in the past; (2) mentioned as a current and obvious support; (3) mentioned as "key" or "critical," or clearly emphasized over other support sources. Of the 44 teachers[1] with advisors who responded to the question, 34 made significant reference to advisors, as indicated by a 2 or 3 rating. The next most supportive influence was "other teachers," a resource mentioned as significant by 14 teachers. The principal and the aide tied for the third major support source, each being mentioned in a significant way by 12 teachers. Thus, advisors were singled out over twice as much as the next three most frequently mentioned sources of support. Whether advisors continued to play such an influential role in these teachers' development is an open question, but it seems clear that the advisor was a salient influence in the first two or three years of attempting to implement a more open approach.

In their perception of advisors as "supportive," what kinds of support did the teachers mean? What did they have in mind when they mentioned advisors in response to the summary evaluation question above? Simple generalizations are not applicable here, for the teachers meant many different things.

[1] Forty-six teachers actually had advisors, but in two cases the interview had to be terminated before the last three questions were asked. Fourteen teachers who had no advisor are not included in this particular analysis.

We began the second portion of the interview (the working environment section) with an extensive discussion of the advisory. We asked how teachers got into the advisory program in the first place, what their skepticisms were initially and what they continued to be skeptical about, how the program operated and how they interacted with advisors, what seemed particularly helpful in the advisors' activities as well as what seemed obstructive, how the program might be improved, and so on. Several coding schemes were devised and applied to the interview data regarding advisors, but the heart of the coding related to the teachers' perceptions of support.

KINDS OF PERCEIVED SUPPORT FROM ADVISORS

What advisors actually do to assist and support teachers covers a wide range of activities and, of course, varies considerably from advisor to advisor and from school to school, with different schools offering different possibilities and constraints for advisors. One typical way in which the advisors operated at the time the study was conducted, however, was to go into a classroom and actually work with a child or group of children. The following excerpts illustrate the wide range of perceptions that teachers had of this type of advising.

1. "Yes, the advisors came to the classroom last year." ["For what purpose?"] "Well, they work right with the children, evidently to see if you're having any difficulty. I don't know—they've never said to me 'You seem to be having a problem,' or anything like that. They would write something with the children, or read a story with them, or make something—right in there with whatever the children were doing at the time. They talked to me once about a project in the room, but I really never discussed much with them." ["Have you asked them in this year?"] "No—I assumed that like last year they would be around to classrooms."

2. "We wanted help in how to make the whole day integrated. The advisors would come in and do one little thing, and you knew they were thinking I should 'see how well it works.' But then you have a whole day of 'see how well it works' with yourself—and it didn't work so well! . . . I want the advisors to run the classroom for a day so I can know what to do."

139

3. "I'm not very good at extending on the spur of the moment, but the advisor is great at this—especially in nature and science. I'd like him to come in every day and work with the kids. He'll go in and start fiddling around with something and have a group of kids interested, and I wouldn't know enough to start fiddling around with it in the first place. I feel he can add something that I *can't* to my classroom."

4. "Oh, yes, they come right in the room and work. And when they're there, they usually do something I wouldn't have thought of . . . and I try to jot it down so I can remember to do it later."

5. "They would come into the room and do something with the children, or we'd all go out on a field trip and bring something back and develop it. This year, the advisor's style is very different from that. She comes into the room very much as an observer and feeds back what she sees to you later. I feel very close to my previous advisors as people, but their type of advising, for me at least, was too much here today and gone tomorrow—because I wasn't sufficiently able to pick up on the leads they had given me. . . . So it was a beautiful thing while they were there, but when they left it was over. I couldn't make it sustained. Maybe now, but then it just didn't gel enough."

6. "When she sits down to work with one of my kids—if I'm lucky enough to have time to watch—that's how you learn from a master teacher. It really is. I would never give it up . . . ."

7. "Her way of working is the best way I learn. She'll come in the room—look around—then maybe discuss things with me a few minutes. Then she'll sit down and work with some children, and she'll talk in a *very loud voice* so I can hear without having to stop what I'm doing. I literally learned how to talk and work with children in new ways from listening to her."

On occasion, advisors would work in a classroom for the sole purpose of providing another pair of hands to help a teacher. In general, however, working in a classroom was intended in the broadest sense as a "modeling" activity, to provide the teacher with leads and ideas about ways of interacting with children and ways of extending the curriculum to build on children's interests. Depending upon the personality of a particular advisor and the receptivity of a particular teacher, it seems obvious that advisors did vary in the extent to which they explicitly discussed their activities in the classroom with teachers. But such variation in operating styles does not seem sufficient to explain the enormous differences in teachers' perceptions of this activity. Theoretically, these differences are attributable to a combination of factors, including as most important: (1) how a teacher construes the advisor's behavior, and (2) the teacher's perception of self-needs, which in turn is related to (3) a particular stage of evolving understanding of what it means to "teach informally."

In order to portray differences in perception of advisors' activities, a coding scheme was derived directly from comments made during the advisory section of the interview. To be eligible for coding, a statement had to indicate clearly that a particular activity had some impact on the teacher and was not merely a description of what advisors were doing in the school. Comments were then coded differentially so as to distinguish between positive perceptions of a supportive activity (+); perceptions of an activity that the teacher recognized as potentially supportive but was not able to draw upon (0); and perceptions of supportive activities that the teacher wanted but was not getting or was not getting "enough of"—in other words, an expression of some kind of discontent (*). The coding scheme thus differentiated between a category or type of activity the teacher perceived an advisor to be engaged in, and whether or not that activity was considered supportive. This differential coding may be illustrated by examining key comments in the excerpts presented previously.

1. "Yes, the advisors came to the classroom last year." ["For what purpose?"] "Well, they work right with the children, evidently to see if you're having any difficulty."

This excerpt, in its entirety, was not considered eligible for coding either as a complaint, as a positive perception of support, or as potential support. In fact, throughout her total interview, this teacher gave little evidence of understanding what the advisors were trying to do. The only thing that was clear was that she kept advisors at arms' length, attending only those workshops that she perceived were "required" by the school administration. She was one of two teachers in the sample who fell outside the coding scheme, so to speak, and who were finally coded as *No Supportive Perception: Advisors are still seen as supervisory figures who are checking up on the teacher, and they are perceived as vaguely threatening.*

2. "We wanted help in how to make the whole day integrated. The advisors would come in and do one little thing, and you knew they were thinking I should 'see how well it works.' But then you have a whole day of 'see how well it works' with yourself—and it didn't work so well! . . . I want the advisors to run the classroom for a day so I can know what to do."

This teacher clearly did not want modeling activity in the broadest sense, nor is that what she perceived the advisors were doing. Rather, she perceived them as demonstrating "one little thing" that she might copy, and the "one little thing" was hardly sufficient for carrying through the whole day. What this teacher wanted and felt she was not getting was specific direction in "what to do." Thus, this excerpt was coded as a discontent perception (*) in the category of activity labeled *Stage Director/ Demonstrator*.

3. "I'm not very good at extending on the spur of the moment, but the advisor is great at this—especially in nature and science. . . . I feel he can add something that I *can't* to my classroom."

Here, the intended modeling activity was perceived as a "helping out" activity in the sense of having another teacher in the classroom. This excerpt was coded as a positive supportive perception (+) in the category labeled *Extension of Teacher*.

4. "Oh, yes, they come right in the room and work. And when they're there, they usually do something I wouldn't have thought of . . . and I try to jot it down so I can remember to do it later."

Again, the intended modeling activity was not perceived as such by this teacher, but was perceived as a specific demonstration of something she might do in exactly the way the advisors had done it. Thus, this excerpt was coded as a positive supportive perception (+) in the *Stage Director/Demonstrator* category.

5. "They would come into the room and do something with the children, or we'd all go out on a field trip and bring something back and develop it. . . . I feel very close to my previous advisors as people, but their type of advising, for me at least, was too much here today and gone tomorrow— because I wasn't sufficiently able to pick up on the leads they had given me. . . . Maybe now, but then it just didn't gel enough."

This teacher did perceive the intention behind the advisors' activities as being a modeling intention and not a demonstration of something she should "copy." At that point in her development, however, she could not "pick up on the leads they had given me." Her excerpt was coded as perceiving an activity as potentially supportive but not being able to draw upon it (0) in the category labeled *Modeling Agent.* Her comment was one of the few (0) codings within the *Modeling Agent* category, and she was an unusually perceptive teacher in her observations of advisors as well as in her observations of her own development. That is, she could analyze and separate her own developmental needs from what she perceived the advisors were trying to accomplish. In contrast, most other teachers construed this particular activity of working with children in the classroom either as it was intended by the advisors or in ways that were dictated by their own needs—and they found it helpful or not.

6. "When she sits down to work with one of my kids—if I'm lucky enough to have time to watch—that's how you learn from a master teacher."

7. "Her way of working is the best way I learn. . . . I literally learned how to talk and work with children in new ways from listening to her."

In both excerpts, the teachers clearly perceived the advisors' activity as a kind of modeling behavior, and they were both able to gain from it. Thus, both excerpts were coded as supportive perceptions (+) in the *Modeling Agent* category.

These examples have been used to illustrate how a single kind of activity (in this case, working with children in the classroom) was construed in different ways by teachers. Although other activities, such as providing the teacher with materials, did not usually elicit several diverse interpretations, most of the teachers tended to perceive the advisors' actions in more than one way. As another example, when teachers sought advice and consultation from advisors, some regarded this interaction as obtaining a specific solution to a specific problem, whereas others gleaned more generalized principles from consulting. In the first instance, the teacher was coded as perceiving the advisor in a supportive role of *Diagnostician and Problem-Solver*; in the second instance, the coding reflected a perception of the advisor as an *Explainer and Theorist.* In all, 13 different categories of perceived support were identified. The 12 categories used in the final analyses of the data are presented in Table 19.

Table 19

Coding Scheme: Perception of Support from Advisors[1]

X. *No Supportive Perception:* Advisors are still seen as supervisory figures who are checking up on the teacher, and they are perceived as vaguely threatening.

Advisor Perceived As:

A. *Service and Administrative Agent*

- brings, makes, or orders materials for teacher.
- reimburses expenses or arranges time off for educational purposes.
- acts as buffer between teacher and administration or parents in explaining program.
- acts as buffer with administration in settling problems (e.g., custodial complaints).

B. *Extension of Teacher* (helping hand; parallel activity)

- works with children in the classroom.
- helps teacher with the room arrangement.
- helps teacher make materials.
- works with children in the corridor or in the resource room.

C. *Emotional Stabilizer and Stimulator*

- provides reinforcement for teacher.
- is a morale booster.
- is a sympathetic listener, someone who "cares."
- inspires sense of group-belonging and purpose.

---

[1]This coding scheme does not include remarks about workshops. The examples shown are illustrative and not exhaustive of a category.

Table 19 (continued)

Coding Scheme: Perception of Support from Advisors

Advisor Perceived As:

D. *Respecter of Individuality*

- understands teacher's perspective.

- knows teacher's room and what teacher is trying to accomplish.

- accepts teacher's goals and present level of development.

- respects individual ways of doing things.

E. *Stage Director and Demonstrator* (teacher's apparent intent is to "copy" what advisor does or transmit an idea directly into the classroom)

- shows teacher how to work with children.

- shows teacher what to do/what not to do (specific direction and criticism).

- shows teacher how to use materials.

- shows teacher how to set up room.

- determines teacher's needs and points out next steps.

- suggests specific ideas that teacher follows literally (e.g., scheduling day).

F. *Diagnostician and Problem-solver*

- teacher receives advice on specific problems (e.g., how to handle a particular child, how to "revitalize" an area in the room).

- teacher is able to pinpoint a problem not previously perceived after consultation with advisor; once problem is identified, the solution seems apparent and teacher regards problem as more or less "over."

Table 19 (continued)

Coding Scheme: Perception of Support from Advisors

Advisor Perceived As:

G. *Provider of Alternatives*

- teacher receives new ideas for instructional activity, but retains responsibility (implicitly or explicitly) for selecting a particular idea and deciding upon an appropriate time, place, and manner for trying it out.

H. *Explainer and Theorist*

- explains educational principles.

- explains reasons for specific actions with children.

- provides theoretical rationale for open education.

- provides literature on open education and discusses it with the teacher.

I. *Modeling Agent*

- teacher infers general principles or patterns of new behavior by observing the advisor interact with children over materials or with other teachers over classroom or school issues.

J. *Appreciative Critic and Discussant*

- teacher gains insights from a thoughtful analysis of the classroom provided by an observer whom the teacher judges knowledgeable and understanding.

- in-depth discussion with advisor leads to new ideas or insights.

K. *Provocative and Reflective Agent*

- advisor's questions stimulate thought.

- discussion leads to teacher's awareness of self-progress.

- advisor helps teacher come to identify self-needs and priorities.

- "bouncing ideas off advisor" and "playing with ideas" in discussion leads to clarification and crystalizing of teacher's thought.

Table 19 (continued)

Coding Scheme: Perception of Support from Advisors

Advisor Perceived As:

L. *Leader and Challenger*

- stimulates new efforts and ways of doing things on teacher's part (e.g., keeping anecdotal records and analyzing samples of children's work).

- provides model of a person who can rationally challenge arbitrary decisions; leads teacher to see himself capable of doing this when necessary.

The category that was dropped for purposes of data analysis was one labeled *Social/Philosophical Change Agent.* This category primarily involved perceptions of advisors as instrumental in establishing new patterns of relationship within the school, or in changing educational priorities within the school and community. Since influence that spreads to the larger educational community was a desired goal of the advisory programs, it is unfortunate that lack of comparability between sites forced our decision to eliminate the category from the final analyses. The problem in coding resulted from the fact that teachers apparently meant very different things when they referred to changing patterns of relationships and changing priorities. In New York City, for example, this perception ranged from totally new relationships between teachers in a school, to beginning changes in parent or administrative understandings of what schools should be doing for children, to perceived support for young, idealistic teachers. In the Follow Through sites, on the other hand, social change perceptions often focused on the medical and social service components of the federal Follow Through program. Similarly, when parent changes were mentioned at one Follow Through site, it usually meant a change in the direction of parents taking an interest in the schools that they had not evidenced before (not necessarily a change in ideas about what schools should do), or of parents banding together for the first time to fight for the continuation of Follow Through monies from Washington. Although these matters are highly significant, they tended not to be comparable from site to site, and it was extremely difficult to determine the degree to which teachers *associated* changes with the presence of the advisory program or actually *attributed* the changes to the programs.

GENERAL RESULTS: PERCEPTION OF SUPPORT CODING

Interpretation of the "perception of support" coding is more complicated than curriculum coding or child coding. In the curriculum chapter, for instance, we dealt with instructional priorities and understandings that could be interpreted in terms of our own theoretical position and of philosophical constructs underlying open education. Similarly, general theoretical assumptions about children's resources served as a basis both for constructing and interpreting the child coding schemes. As can be seen, however, the perception of support coding was derived more on an empirical basis, from what teachers actually said. Although a theoretical framework for analyzing perceptions of support will be developed later in the chapter, it should be noted that these data are more confounded than data from the curriculum/child portion of the interview in two important respects. Not only do the data mirror differences in individual construct systems, but they also reflect (1) differences in site conditions together with differences in the complexity of advising at different sites, and (2) differences between advisors in style and mode of advising.

Because of these confounding influences, generalizations about the group of teachers as a whole are more difficult to make and should be regarded as somewhat tentative in nature. Given this precaution, we nevertheless can point to some general results of the perception of support coding.

Pervasive individual differences in construing a particular advising activity were illustrated by the excerpts given in the opening pages of this chapter. These differences constitute a major finding of the study. The practical implications of this finding, however, are not entirely clear. It may be that advisors should be more explicit about their intentions when they work with teachers. Yet any pronouncement like "I'm working with children in your classroom to provide you with a general model of teaching behavior and not specific examples of something you should copy" is hardly called for, nor would it be especially effective. Indeed, it might well result in a swift invitation to leave the classroom. Perhaps all that can be said at the present time is that the finding itself—that teachers perceive the same advisor activity in different ways—helps to clarify one of the subtle difficulties of both advising and teaching.

RESULTS OF THE (0) CODING, REFLECTING INABILITY TO BENEFIT FROM AN ADVISOR'S ACTIVITY

Nine teachers gave 14 responses that were classified as (0) or "can't benefit" codings. Since this represents less than 3 percent of a total of 474 codable comments, these responses have been eliminated from all other major analyses and are only presented here. (The total perception of support responses given in subsequent analyses is 460.) The 14 responses in question were distributed over the various support categories as follows:

Support Category	*Number of Responses Coded (0)*
A. Service and Administrative Agent	1
B. Extension of Teacher	2
E. Stage Director and Demonstrator	5
G. Provider of Alternatives	2
H. Explainer and Theorist	1
I. Modeling Agent	3

One teacher who gave a (0) response in both the A and E categories was the only person in the study who consistently assumed a posture of not needing the help of advisors. On the other hand, she was also consistent during the first portion of the interview in her vague perception of connections between her curriculum priorities and the rather rich surface curriculum she had provided in the classroom.

The remaining four (0) codings in the E category stemmed from somewhat different perceptions. Two teachers felt that a specific suggestion offered by their respective advisors had been too difficult to carry out. The other two E responses focused on the repetitious nature of suggestions they received. That is, some suggestions that had proved helpful during their initial year in the program were being repeated and were no longer perceived as very useful. We suspect that this is actually an underestimate of the number of teachers who felt that certain suggestions were repetitious, since several teachers hinted at this type of criticism. That they did not come out more strongly and actually complain about it was not a matter of politeness, we believe, because they generally were not hesitant to express discontent about other things. Rather, they probably did not complain because they perceived it as a benefit for "newcomers to the program." In general, suggestions repeated by advisors apparently were for the benefit of newcomers, but occasionally they were offered by advisors who were new to a school. In any event, the problem of

149

repetition is a very real one and is recognized as such by most advisory and workshop personnel with whom we have worked. In the long run, it is a problem that must be faced and resolved in some way by all advisory and workshop groups.

The two teachers who gave "can't benefit" responses in category G seemed inconsistent in that they also reported supportive perceptions in the G category. The single (0) coding in the *Explainer and Theorist* category came from a teacher who felt frustrated by advisors on almost every count and who gave 4 of the 14 (0) responses. Yet she was also a teacher who perceived value in the educational idea fostered by the advisory program and who was attempting to implement the idea as best she could.

The category I *(Modeling Agent)* responses were all of the nature illustrated in excerpt #5. That is, the teachers felt they were not at a point in their development where they could "pick up" on the modeling behavior of advisors. Although these data are sketchy, to say the least, this last finding is suggestive when combined with the fact that several teachers perceived intended modeling behavior as "extra help in the classroom" and were coded in category B *(Extension of Teacher).* It may be that modeling is an effective support activity for many teachers only when they are beyond the initial stages of understanding an open approach to teaching. On the other hand, most advisory programs would not advocate a modeling strategy for experienced teachers who had already developed their own style of open teaching. Modeling, in the final analysis, must be an "in-between" or "it depends" strategy that calls for sensitive judgment on the part of advisors.

The final two (0) codings were in the *Extension of Teacher* category. One of these responses was simply a matter of a teacher who felt that an additional person helping in the classroom was not really necessary. The other (0) response was more interesting and came from a teacher who talked a great deal about the support she had received during the previous year from observing advisors work in her classroom (i.e., *modeling* support). She went on to say that the school had converted one of the classrooms to a "resource room" during the course of the current year, and that advisors with special talents in such areas as pottery or creative writing would work with children in the resource room. As she put it,

> "They take the kids out [of the classroom] to work with them, so I don't see anything. I guess they feel they can reach more kids that way, but they're not helping me."

This last illustration muddies the issue, of course, because it clearly indicates that some teachers can and do gain support during their initial year in the program from observing advisors work with children in the classroom. It also reinforces the idea that the wisdom of modeling must be judged by advisors on an individual basis.

Although the 14 (0) responses point to some interesting issues, the primary result of this coding analysis is the overall infrequency of (0) responses. Generally speaking, there are few things advisors do that are perceived in an "I can't benefit from it" manner. The vast majority of advising activity is perceived as directly impinging on the teacher in some way.

RESULTS OF THE EMOTIONAL SUPPORT CODING

One of the most striking impressions from conducting the interview study was the degree to which teachers welcomed the opportunity to talk about teaching in all of its facets—from their aspirations and successes to their failures, anxieties, and problems. As mentioned previously a great many teachers continued the "interview" even after the tape recorder had been turned off.

This general impression that teachers valued an interested listener was not only borne out but greatly expanded in coding the Advisory section of the interview. Approximately one-fourth to one-third of all perception of support responses *at each site* fell within the two emotional support categories (category C: *Emotional Stabilizer and Stimulator;* and category D: *Respecter of Individuality*). Fewer responses were coded in category D than in C, since D generally indicated perception of emotional support at a more selective and differentiated level than C statements. In essence, D responses were tantamount to teachers saying that they appreciated a phenomenological approach on the part of the advisor, and some went on to make the direct connection between an advisor's approach to teachers and a teacher's approach to children.

> "It depends on the attitude. If an advisor sees herself as an enabler of teachers, just like a teacher sees herself as an enabler of children, then you're in good shape. That's really where it's at."

> "Advisors have to be practical and realize that teachers are individuals and approach the program differently. What's good is that advisors look at teachers as they expect teachers to look at children."

151

Regardless of the category in which a particular response was coded, many responses indicated a clear distinction between the type of emotional support and reinforcement received from advisors and the type of support previously received from supervisors. The following excerpts illustrate a variety of perceptions of emotional support.

"Teachers working in structured classrooms don't get this kind of support, and they need it too. All they have is a supervisor coming in and telling them 'what songs to teach this week'—and that's no help. It's a warmer atmosphere now, and you don't feel you're alone doing this big job."
[coded C category]

"We try to tune in to kids—who they are, where they are, what they are—and you have to get the same kind of thing from the advisory. Otherwise it's just another supervisor coming in and saying 'everything's fine, but why don't you try that other little game?' These games and gimmicks—I don't believe in any of that stuff plucked from thin air."
[coded D category]

"I get the feeling from my advisor and other people in the program that they're *on my side*—they're interested in helping solve my problems. And that's important!"
[coded C category]

"What's most helpful is an advisor following up on your room, because it's important to get to know your room. It's great to have a person who has a good relationship with you—someone who really gets to know your room, and you, and what you're about!"
[coded D category]

"At first I didn't want anyone in the classroom watching me. But the advisors never made me feel that they were above me in the sense of never making mistakes. . . . The advisors treat everyone decently. They're there to help you do the best job you can and not to criticize everything. They're also interested in the children. . . . I'm not afraid of them any more—I like the advisors coming into the room."
[coded C category]

"The advisor isn't like a 'boss.' I can relate what's going wrong. Like I can say, 'It's been a horrible day—talk to me!' . . . There's very close communication with the advisor and we're often on the phone for hours. It's a high level of relationship—of interaction and communication—between children and teachers, between teachers and teachers, and between teachers and the advisor. That's what's so very nice about being part of the program."

[coded C category]

"I've heard many positive comments from lots of people that I didn't value (although it's great to hear)—because I felt these people were not seeing my room. But the advisor used to come in and work with children, and she *would* get the feeling of the room. She could pick up on something I might not have seen. . . . It's very important to have a relationship of mutual respect."

[coded D category]

We have illustrated what teachers had to say about emotional support at some length because we believe that their remarks highlight a concern that may be conspicuous by its absence in the usual life of a school.

RESULTS OF THE (*) CODING, REFLECTING TEACHER DISCONTENT

Even though most of the teachers viewed their advisory program as supportive in general, they did not hesitate to express discontent with the advisory when they thought their discontent was legitimate. Some questions in the interview were intended to probe for areas where teachers felt that improvement was needed in the program or where drastic changes were called for. No one came up with recommendations for drastic changes, and significant discontent tended to surface before we ever got around to probing for suggested improvements.

Eighty-four of the 460 perception of support responses (18%) were coded as reflecting some degree of discontent, and the remaining 82 percent were coded as positive support perceptions. The discontent referred to a supportive activity that teachers wanted but perceived they were not getting, or a particular kind of activity they wanted "more of." Thus, the discontent remarks ranged from anger and frustration at perceived gaps in advisory service to comments that were in the spirit of wanting more of something that was liked. Whatever the nature of the remark, however, it was generally expressed with a firmness and conviction that belied any expectancy that complaints were "unacceptable."

In analyzing the discontent codings for any generalized patterns, we considered only those categories that drew responses from

50 percent or more of the teachers at each site, in order to avoid spurious comparisons. With this restriction on the analysis, one pattern that held up across all sites was that category D (*Respecter of Individuality*) drew proportionately more discontent perceptions than any other category. That is, the ratio of discontent responses to total responses was consistently higher than for any other category, ranging from 21 percent at one site to 50 percent at another and averaging 39 percent overall. Category C (*Emotional Stabilizer and Stimulator*), on the other hand, received few discontent responses compared to other categories at each site, and at two sites there were no discontent perceptions at all in category C.

After what has just been said about emotional support, this finding with respect to category D seems incongruous at first glance. Actually, however, it is not so incongruous when viewed in the light of teachers' actual comments, of the philosophic emphasis of the programs, and of the difficulty of being a D person with everyone. In the first place, all of the teachers had had contact with more than one advisor; and many supportive D perceptions regarding a particular advisor were contrasted with the lack of D qualities in another advisor. The following excerpts are typical of what teachers said in contrasting advisors on the quality of *Respecter of Individuality*.

> "It depends on who the advisor is. Last year I would have given you totally different answers because last year's advisor wasn't particularly helpful—wasn't really tuned in to where the teacher was. And *that's* where it goes awry. If an advisor wants you to do her thing—to run your classroom her kind of way, because she can't cope with your way—she can't get her head to where yours is at—then it's no good. 'Cause that's only one more hurdle, one more hassle, one more burden. . . ."

> "There's a tremendous difference in the amount of help advisors give. Last year, the advisor was not really giving teachers what they wanted. She didn't know what to give them because she didn't realize they really wanted to see her in their rooms. We wanted to get feedback from her on, 'Am I moving towards my goals?' My advisor this year, of course, understood that teachers needed that kind of help and [she gave it]. . . ."

This type of direct comparison between advisors was rarely made with respect to category C, as the great majority of C perceptions were positive in nature. Likewise, teachers seldom compared advisors in terms of the perceptions reflected by the other support categories.

Aside from this comparative bent, the teachers displayed another unique response tendency in category D. Thirty of the 46 teachers with advisors gave one or more responses that were coded as D. These 30 teachers were distributed as follows:

14 - positive support perception(s) only
9 - positive and discontent perception(s)
7 - discontent perception(s) only

The unique tendency is represented by the 7 teachers who had only discontent perceptions. This same coding (discontent only) occurred only 8 times for all of the other 11 categories combined. In other words, most teachers did not exhibit discontent about something that they did not also experience as positive support. We suspect that a disproportionate number of teachers (those making comparisons on D and those giving only discontent D responses) were highly sensitized to the presence or absence of *respecting individuality* because this was such a central tenet of the advisory program philosophy.

To expand this argument a bit more, respecting *children's* individuality was high on the list of priorities that the advisory programs were trying to foster. It seems only natural, then, that teachers would be quite conscious of the manner in which this priority was carried out (or not carried out) in an advisor's approach to them. Holding the ideal of respect and being able to communicate respect are two different matters, however, and apparently not all advisors were capable of communicating this quality as effectively as they may have wished. By way of contrast, if the advisory programs we studied had placed a high priority on teachers' diagnosing and solving children's problems, and if the teachers in the programs had accepted this priority, one might expect a disproportionate number of teachers to have been sensitized to the presence or absence of category F (*Diagnostician and Problem Solver*) support from advisors.

The category that received the second highest proportion of discontent perceptions at all sites but one was category E (*Stage Director and Demonstrator*). This finding is not surprising because it is the type of support that many advisors are rather reluctant to provide. This, of course, does not mean they don't provide it. Advisors recognize the necessity of giving teachers (particularly new teachers) some specific direction in such things as how to set up the classroom and how to use various materials with children. They are hesitant to keep up this role for long, however, for it often appears to promote dependence and to undercut their aim of helping teachers become self-sufficient in adapting the environment and the curriculum to meet the needs of individual chidren.

A third generalization that comes from the analysis of the discontent coding has to do with support category G (*Provider of Alternatives*). This category received proportionately *fewer* discontent responses than any other category that was mentioned by more than half of the teachers at each site. Specifically, the ratio of discontent to total responses coded in the G category at each site ranged from 0 percent to 7 percent. Yet *Provider of Alternatives* received the highest percentage of all support responses given by teachers at two sites and was among the most popular categories at the other two sites. In short, the advisors at all sites were perceived as providing a sufficiency of instructional alternatives, so that very few teachers complained about not receiving this type of support or not receiving enough of it. This result is interesting because it indicates what seems to be a basic strength and strategy of all the advisory groups. That is, suggesting alternatives is a type of supportive activity that most advisors like to engage in, and it is one that most of them are well equipped to provide.

It could be argued that all of the categories from E (*Stage Director and Demonstrator*) through L (*Leader and Challenger*) embody the idea of providing instructional alternatives, and this is undoubtedly true. However, it has already been pointed out that the majority of advisors try to avoid any intensive role of *Stage Director,* and the remaining categories reflect ways of suggesting alternatives that require varying degrees of special understanding, interpersonal sensitivity, and diplomacy. Most of the comments coded as G support perceptions, on the other hand, referred to obtaining instructional ideas via the more commonplace route of one-to-one conversations with the advisor or of small group meetings at lunch or after school. Although the advisory groups undoubtedly did contain unusually talented individuals among their number—people with a high degree of understanding, sensitivity, and diplomacy—unusual talent was evidently not the criterion of being reasonably capable of providing teachers with alternative ideas about instruction. The only apparent requirements were having the ideas in the first place and being able to communicate them.

That providing alternatives represented a common strength and strategy of the advisory groups is further supported by the fact that the category G finding (i.e., few discontent perceptions) runs counter to the fourth and last generalization that can be made about the discontent coding. Exclusive of the two emotional support categories and with the exception of category G, the support categories that teachers mentioned most frequently at each site were also the categories that received the most discontent or "want more of" responses. This last result is understandable in the sense that people tend to want "more of" something that is perceived as helpful and supportive. The nature of the most frequently mentioned support categories differed from site to site, however, and reflected differing conditions and circumstances between sites.

MEDIATION OF SUPPORT

Although the generalizations discussed in the previous section highlight a number of issues, the question of perceived support is perhaps more meaningfully asked within the context of what the advisors were trying to accomplish. Despite their different strategies and logistics, all the advisory programs shared the goal of helping teachers assume a more thoughtful and active role in influencing the educational environment. It follows, then, that their ultimate aim was not to provide isolated services or singular solutions to a particular problem, but to provide a range of support that would enable teachers to analyze situations and arrive at their own decisions about problems and solutions to them. Thus, the advisors' long-range goal was to perform an educative function, a goal discussed at some length in Chapter 2. Given this purpose, the notion of mediated support—support in which the receiver plays an active part—becomes critical.

In everyday usage, *mediation* usually brings to mind a picture of labor and management negotiations, and the word has a specialized meaning in psychology that is derived from the behaviorist tradition. We intend neither of these meanings. Nevertheless, we need a term to designate differences between people in how they construe themselves vis-à-vis the environment—as shapers of external influences or as consumers of external influences. Perhaps *mediation* is not the best choice of words to imply this distinction, but other phrases that come to mind ("inner-outer directed," for example) have been overworked in recent years and connote too broad a range of meanings.

Excluding perceptions of emotional support (categories C and D), the ordering of the other support categories reflects a general progression from what is basically a consumer orientation to a more mediating stance on the part of the teacher. That is, the first few categories suggest a more receptive, "taking in" relationship to advisor support, with the teacher doing little in the way of reformulating the experience. The latter categories, on the other hand, suggest a more active role by the teacher in terms of self-investment, critical judgment, inference, conceptual reorganization, or other ways of contributing to the supportive activities of the advisors. This general progression, however, is not to be judged as running from "bad to good" with respect to what advisors (or others in a supportive role) *actually do*. They can increase a teacher's knowledge by demonstrating how to use materials (category E), they can smooth over initial rough spots by helping a teacher rearrange the classroom (category B), and they can provide a better climate for teacher experimentation by obtaining materials and by acting as a buffer with the administration or parents (category A) when that is necessary. Over time, however, advisors would hope to see teachers who entered the program with a consumer orientation toward support move to a more active role in mediating their own development. This is not to imply that all teachers entered the advisory programs with a basically passive view of support. It seemed clear that many did not. One teacher, for example, talked about her previous experience in a school where the principal had "squelched" her efforts to open up the classroom. In commenting on her entry into the advisory program, she said:

> "There were no excuses here, because I had all kinds of support available from the advisors. I knew my success or failure as a teacher would depend very much on me . . . and that was pretty scary."

In attempting to refine the concept of mediation for purposes of data analysis, we formulated a rationale based on three psychological processes: (1) internalization, (2) selection, and (3) integration. These processes are reflected in the support categories in varying degrees, as shown in the following groupings (categories C and D are excluded):

Support Categories Grouped by Degree of Mediation

A. Service and Administrative Agent
B. Extension of Teacher

> Support in these categories was perceived primarily as an external service and not as a psychological or educational input. Thus, these categories do not reflect the first process of *internalization*.

E. Stage Director and Demonstrator

F. Diagnostician and Problem-Solver

>Here, support was *internalized* to the extent that the teacher could articulate some specific idea, strategy, or method that he or she had received from an advisor. There was little evidence, however, that the teacher had been *selective* in determining what to "take in."

G. Provider of Alternatives

H. Explainer and Theorist

>By definition, alternatives and theoretical principles are selectively retained. Thus, these categories reflect a *selective internalization* of ideas and information. However, there was little evidence from comments coded in these categories that the ideas and information gained from advisors had been integrated with other of the teacher's thoughts.

I. Modeling Agent

J. Appreciative Critic and Discussant

K. Provocative and Reflective Agent

L. Leader and Challenger

>In order to be coded in these categories, a remark had to reflect not only selective internalization, but an *integration* with other ideas. There was evidence that the teacher had given "shape" to the ideas and thoughts that came out of an interaction with an advisor and had made those ideas and thoughts his own. In other words, there was evidence of inference, critical judgment, and/or conceptual reorganization on the teacher's part.

To summarize, we have considered categories A and B as being nonmediated support and categories E through L as being mediated support, with E and F reflecting minimal mediation, G and H reflecting a middle-level mediation, and I through L reflecting maximal mediation. In order to derive a mediation index for each teacher, perception of support responses were weighted differentially: A and B responses received a weight of 0; E and F responses received a weight of 1; G and H responses, a weight of 2; and I, J, K, and L responses, a weight of 3. Emotional support responses (categories C and D) were not included in calculating the mediation index. The following hypothetical example shows a distribution of responses over the various support categories and illustrates how the mediation index was derived.

	Nonmediated and Emotional Support Categories				Mediated Support Categories			Mediation Index
	A	B	C	D	E,F	G,H	I,J,K,L	
Number of Teacher Responses	2	1	3	2	4	2	1	
					x 1	x 2	x 3	
					4 +	4 +	3	= 11

Since it would be difficult at best to generalize about mediation of support across the varying conditions at different sites, it seemed a more useful approach to look at mediation in relation to the teachers' receptivity to advisors. We say "receptivity to *advisors*" and not "to the advisory program" for two reasons. First, the advisors *were* the program insofar as some teachers were concerned, for they appeared to have only vague understandings of any larger program effort. Second, the advisors embodied the program for many practical purposes, and a teacher who was not receptive to the advisors had few other sources of support in this approach to teaching. All teachers, of course, were encouraged to work with and to support each other, but at the time of the study most teachers were not experienced enough themselves to provide much beyond emotional support and help with the "fundamentals."

An initial grouping of teachers was based on two global ratings that provided a reasonable index of receptivity: general feelings toward the advisors (including whether these feelings were emphatic or nonemphatic) and the amount of use of advisory services (e.g., frequency of attendance at workshops given or sponsored by the advisory groups). These combined indices plus a general review of the content of teachers' remarks (not counting the perception of support comments) led to four different groups. Group 1 teachers (N = 11) appeared to view the advisors as not only highly salient but also critical influences in their professional development. For Group 2 teachers (N = 10), the advisors were judged to be important and salient influences, but clearly not as critical as for Group 1 teachers. Teachers in Group 3 (N = 18) could best be described as accepting and even welcoming the advisors, but on the whole they did not talk about advisors as especially salient influences in their teaching lives. Group 4 teachers (N = 5) expressed varying degrees of negative attitudes toward the advisors. The two teachers who were coded as having "No Supportive Perceptions" were eliminated from this analysis, thus reducing the sample to 44 teachers. Although Groups 1 and 2 were the most receptive to advisors, the importance of advisor support in the teachers' development did not preclude their expressing any critical or discontent remarks, as the following figures indicate.

Receptivity Group	N	Percentage of Discontent Support Perceptions
1	11	15
2	10	11
3	18	11
4	5	60
	44	

Tables 20 and 21 depict differences between receptivity groups in perception of advisor support. Table 20 shows the percentage of teachers in each receptivity group who gave responses coded in the various support categories. Table 21 presents the average number of responses in different support categories for teachers in each receptivity group, as well as the average mediation index for each group.

Table 20

Percentage of Teachers in Each Receptivity Group with Support Perceptions Coded in Different Types of Support Categories

Receptivity Group	Percentage in Nonmediated Categories		Percentage in Emotional Support Categories		Percentage in Mediated Categories		
	A	B	C	D	E, F	G, H	I, J, K, L
1. Advisors highly salient and critical for teacher (N = 11)	64	45	64	82	91	91	91
2. Advisors highly salient but not as critical (N = 10)	40	70	80	70	100	80	40
3. Advisors welcomed but not particularly salient (N = 18)	44	55	66	55	78	89	33
4. Mild to strong negative feelings about advisors (N = 5)	80	80	60	80	80	40	20

Table 21

Average Number of Responses in Different Types of Support Categories
and Average Mediation Index for Teachers in
Each Receptivity Group

Receptivity Group	Nonmediated Categories		Emotional Support Categories		Mediated Categories			Average Number of Responses	Average Mediation Index
	A	B	C	D	E,F	G,H	I, J, K,L		
1. (N = 11)	1.3	.8	1.4	2.5	1.9	2.9	3.7	14.5	18.9
2. (N = 10)	.8	1.4	2.4	.9	3.2	1.4	.8	10.9	8.4
3. (N = 18)	.7	.8	1.3	.8	1.7	1.6	.7	7.6	6.9
4. (N = 5)	2.4	1.0	1.2	1.0	3.0	1.2	.6	10.4	7.2

These data are revealing in several respects. First, the average mediation index of 18.9 for Group 1 teachers as compared with the other groups suggests that the advisors were highly successful in promoting and supporting a mediative stance among those teachers who were most receptive to them—approximately one-fourth of all teachers who had advisors. Table 20 further indicates that their success was not just limited to one or two receptive teachers who might have raised the average by providing a great many responses in those categories that received greatest weight in calculating the mediation index (categories I, J, K, and L). Such a spurious result was obviously not the case, as 10 of the 11 Group 1 teachers perceived support in each of the mediated support-category divisions.

Among the strongest correlates of mediation apparent in Table 21 is the type of emotional support valued. Although all the teachers had something to say about category C support, the strongest mediators(Group 1)clearly valued emotional support in the form of advisors respecting their individuality (D category), mentioning this type of support more than twice as frequently as the other teachers. In this sense, the strong mediating teachers took a firm phenomenological position concerning support from advisors, and many made direct analogies to their own work with children. As the teacher quoted previously put it, "We try to tune in to kids—who they are, where they are, what they are—and you have to get the same kind of thing from the advisory."

The advisors appear to have been modestly successful in accomplishing their goal with the rest of the teachers, at least if one interprets the average index for Groups 2, 3, and 4 as reflecting a "modest" degree of mediation. Nonetheless, that they encouraged mediation at all among those who were merely accepting and even negative toward them is somewhat surprising, as is the fact that neither of these last two groups limited their responses to the minimal mediation categories (E and F). In summary, these data seem to indicate that the advisors were modestly to highly successful with the great majority of teachers in accomplishing one of their basic goals—that of encouraging an active, mediative orientation with respect to professional development. It might be hypothesized that these teachers were already realizing their mediative potential before becoming a part of one of the advisory programs, but this is refuted to a considerable degree by their own testimony. Many teachers went on in some detail about the novelty of advisor support. For most, it was a type of encouragement and stimulating relationship that they had not previously encountered in any significant way.

There are, of course, no normative standards by which to judge what is "high" or "low" mediation for teachers-in-general. We can only conjecture on this score. If a recent study by Zahorik (1973) is representative, however, we would guess that mediation for teachers-in-general is fairly low. Zahorik studied 72 midwestern elementary school teachers who were enrolled in graduate classes and pursuing a master's degree in education. As a group, they were mainly urban teachers, and most of them taught at the intermediate rather than at the primary level. Their teaching experience ranged from one or two years to several years. Realizing that there are many constraints on what teachers actually do in the classroom, Zahorik asked the teachers to create fictitious four-page transcripts that would illustrate what they thought their "ideal teaching" would be like. He comments on the analysis of these transcripts as follows:

> The general conclusion that can be drawn from these results is that the teachers in this study had difficulty thinking beyond what they probably do in their classrooms. Their ideal teaching lacked excitement and newness. It showed an alarming absence of either personal reflection concerning what teaching ought to be or operational knowledge of current educational thought. (p. 439)

If graduate courses are considered a potential source of cognitive support, then it would seem that the teachers in Zahorik's study were barely consuming that support, let alone mediating it.

RECEPTIVITY TO ADVISORS AND CONSTRUCTS RELATED TO TEACHING

Providing a context in which teachers mediate support and adopt an active role in shaping the educational environment is a goal of

163

the advisory programs in its own right. This has already been emphasized. It would be a rather vacuous goal, however, if it were conceptually unrelated to other aspects of the educational philosophy shared by the advisory groups. Data from the study indicate that mediation of support is related to other educational understandings, just as the Zahorik study suggests that a nonmediating posture (the absence of personal reflection) is associated with lackluster accounts of "ideal teaching." What is especially noteworthy is the way in which receptivity to advisors and mediation of support appear to be linked to understandings about curriculum and children.

Before discussing this relationship, we should elaborate on a point stated in Chapter 7. The coding and analysis of the working environment portion of the interview (including perception of support from advisors) was accomplished first. The rationale for coding the last portion of the interview first was to be able to provide feedback as quickly as possible to the various advisory groups involved. The rationale for the basic strategy of coding one section of the interview at a time, however, was to reduce "halo effect"—i.e., a coder being influenced in judgments about one portion of the interview from what was heard in the other major portion. Thus, there was an interval of approximately one year between coding and analysis of the working environment section and coding and analysis of the curriculum/child section of the interview. Although these are operational details, we believe they strengthen the evidence with respect to the internal consistency of construct systems and the type of supportive influence that external advisory groups may provide.

In Chapter 4 an analysis was made of teachers' curricular understandings. Our formulation of a curriculum construct system consisted of *surface content* (materials and activities that the teacher plans for children), *organizing content* (the learning priorities that a teacher holds for children), and *connections* between these two components (the clarity with which a teacher perceives that learning priorities are being actualized in the classroom). The organizing priorities were considered to be either narrow, middle-range, or comprehensive in nature, depending on whether they focused exclusively on external behavior or reflected a more holistic concern with children's internal resources. In order to identify different types of construct systems, we considered two basic factors: dominance of the "grade-level facts and skills" priority, and evidence of experimentation with providing a surface curriculum responsive to the interests of individual children. The four resulting groups were described as follows:

164

Group 1. "Grade-level facts and skills" is clearly the dominant priority and there is little evidence of experimentation or change in the surface curriculum from what the teachers had been practicing previously.

Group 2. "Grade-level facts and skills" is clearly the dominant priority, but there is much evidence of change and experimentation with the surface curriculum.

Group 3. "Grade-level facts and skills" is an expressed priority but not the dominant priority. Middle-range priorities tend to be dominant, and there is little evidence of a potentially rich surface curriculum.

Group 4. A comprehensive or middle-range priority is dominant, and there is little evidence of pre-occupation with "grade-level facts and skills" —i.e., it is not codable as such. There is also evidence of a potentially rich surface curriculum.

The percentage of teachers within each of these groups was presented in Chapter 4 for the entire sample. We reproduce those percentages below, as compared with the percentage in each group for the subsample of 46 teachers who were in advisory programs.

Curriculum Group	Percentage Total Sample N = 60	Percentage Advisory Subsample N = 46
Group 1	12	15
Group 2	22	17
Group 3	39	37
Group 4	27	30

As can be seen, no startling shifts take place. The slight rise in Curriculum Group 1 for the advisory sample is due to the fact that the 14 "bootstrap" teachers who were going to workshops were, by definition, experimenting with surface curricular changes. Thus, no "bootstrap" teacher was in Curriculum Group 1. Table 22 shows the relationship between receptivity to advisors and curriculum group.

Table 22

Distribution of Teachers in Receptivity Groups and Curriculum Groups

Receptivity Group		N	Curriculum Group			
			1	2	3	4
1.	Advisors highly salient and critical for teacher	11	-	-	2	9
2.	Advisors highly salient but not as critical	10	-	1	5	4
3.	Advisors welcomed but not particularly salient	18	4	6	7	1
4.	Mild to strong negative feelings about advisors	5	2	-	3	-
X.	No supportive perception	2	1	1	-	-
		46	7	8	17	14

The distributions in Table 22 reveal a strong relationship between receptivity to advisors and curricular understandings that parallel the philosophy of open education. One interesting exception to this general pattern of relationship is represented by the three teachers in Curriculum Group 3 who held negative attitudes towards advisors. Each of these teachers was "sold" on the educational approach represented by the advisory programs, but they were at odds with their particular advisors and highly critical about not receiving enough support, particularly of the *Stage Director/Demonstrator* variety. Two of these three teachers account for another exception to an otherwise clear trend in the data. In Chapter 6, the relationship between phenomenological inquiry and teachers' perceptions of the child-as-resource was analyzed. Table 23 shows the relationship between receptivity to advisors and evidence of phenomenological inquiry.

The reversal of the general trend in Table 23 is accounted for by two of the three teachers in Receptivity Group 4 who were very positive about the advisory program philosophy. The third teacher of this trio was rated high on permeability or "freshness" in her observations of children, even though she gave no evidence of actual phenomenological inquiry into children's perspectives. The remaining two teachers in Receptivity Group 4 showed no signs of permeability.

Table 23

Relationship Between Receptivity to Advisors and Evidence of Phenomenological Inquiry

Receptivity Group		Teachers Coded for Phenomenological Inquiry Within Each Receptivity Group	
	N	N	%
1. Advisors highly salient and critical for teacher	11	9	82
2. Advisors highly salient but not as critical	10	6	60
3. Advisors welcomed but not particularly salient	18	2	11
4. Mild to strong negative feelings about advisors	5	2	40
X. No supportive perception	2	-	—

The picture that begins to emerge from these analyses is a provocative one. First, and most clearly, it indicates that receptivity to advisors is a strong correlate of teaching constructs that closely approximate the open education philosophy. On the other hand, it also suggests that lack of receptivity to advisors per se is not necessarily a handicap in those cases where a teacher is receptive to the educational position that the advisors represent. It is a relatively bland attitude toward advisors and, presumably, toward their educational ideas that seems to pose the most serious obstacle for advisory groups. Although we defined "receptivity" specifically with reference to advisors, these findings make psychological sense. In spite of personal antagonisms, if a teacher values the open education position, advisors may still provide some degree of support. The three teachers in our study who were "exceptions" to general data trends testified to this, as they all reported having received from advisors some ideas and help which they found very useful. If a teacher is lukewarm toward the open education position, however, any amount of support may be relatively ineffectual except with respect to relaxing tensions and creating a more natural and congenial environment in the classroom. Virtually every teacher who had taught traditionally commented on this type of change.

167

This general picture supports two major conclusions. First, commitment to the educational philosophy on the part of the teacher appears essential for the development of understandings that are necessary to implement an open approach. This conclusion may seem obvious at first, but we can readily think of instructional programs that teachers can be conceptually equipped to implement without assuming a necessary commitment to the program philosophy. How personally satisfied teachers might be under such a circumstance or how well they might perform are other questions, but there is little doubt they would be able to understand the "how-to-do-it" of some programs. The second conclusion we draw is that for teachers committed to an open philosophy, the external advisor usually plays a critical role during the initial two or three years in helping them conceptualize an open approach to educating young children. Normally, correlational data of the kind we have presented here do not lend themselves to statements about who influenced whom or what caused what. In this particular case, however, the variable of "Receptivity Group" was based on and defined by the teachers' own statements about the importance of support from advisors.

POSTCRIPT

THE INTERVIEW IN RETROSPECT

In the fall of 1972, one of the authors interviewed eight British teachers who were working in and around the London area. These teachers worked in four different infant schools, all committed to the "integrated day" approach, and they taught populations of children similar to those served by the 60 American teachers. The interview consisted only of the curriculum/child questions, and it lasted approximately one and one-half hours. Although the interview tapes were not formally coded, they were informally judged by four of the six people who had coded the original sample. Our strong impression from these tapes was that the eight British teachers expressed a range of understandings and perceptions equivalent to that of the 60 American teachers. More interesting is the fact that their constructs appeared similar to those of American teachers across the entire range of understandings. Thus, if a British teacher perceived significant resources for learning in children's interests, she tended to talk about "building on interests" in ways reminiscent of what we had heard American teachers say. Similarly, the British teacher who viewed a child's emotional life as something to be "coped with" expressed related perceptions about classroom management and small group work that were clearly recognizable from the original study.

The utility of the interview and of the constructs it elicits has also been tested in a context significantly different from the original research and from the small British study. Specifically, the interview has been employed in an evaluation of a computer-assisted instructional system, PLATO (Programmed Logic for Automatic Teaching Operations). The evaluation, part of another ETS project, is concerned with a field demonstration of curricular materials delivered via interactive computer terminals in elementary and community college classrooms. At the elementary school level, the programmed materials are intended for kindergarten through second-grade reading instruction and fourth-grade through sixth-grade mathematics instruction. These materials are being introduced into nine schools in two districts near the University of Illinois. Altogether, the elementary demonstration involves about 40 teachers. As one component of the evaluation, the teachers who volunteered to have terminals placed in their rooms were interviewed with a somewhat revised form of the original interview instrument. Since the PLATO evaluation is still in progress, final integration of the interview data with several other sources of information about these classrooms is yet to be accomplished. Nevertheless, the interview has already yielded evidence that teachers construe both the value of a computer terminal and the integration of this complex resource with other aspects of their surface curriculum in widely varying ways which, in turn, are related to their curricular priorities and to their perception of children as learners and as resources for teaching.

A third study utilizing modifications of the original procedures is being conducted in Los Angeles under the direction of Professor Elizabeth Brady, California State University, Northridge, California. This evaluation study involves teachers who are participating in a Head Start Primary Continuation Learning Project. To date, the variation in constructs elicited by the interview has been used as an important aspect of the formative evaluation of the project.

Aside from research use, the interview and coding schemes have also been the subject of several graduate and in-service staff development seminars at such places as Creative Teaching Workshop, the Philadelphia Advisory Center, Prospect School, the University of Connecticut, the University of North Dakota, the Greater Boston Teachers Center, and the Workshop Center for Open Education. These discussions have confirmed the pedagogical usefulness of the coding schemes and have helped to sharpen the formulations.

In the spring of 1973, one year after the original interview was conducted, we visited the classrooms of a subsample of 15 teachers in New York City and spent the major part of a day in each classroom. We also reinterviewed the teachers informally. These visits were informative in many respects, but perhaps their primary significance was the opportunity they provided to examine the congruence between constructs inferred from interviewing and from observing the teachers in action. What we saw in the classrooms generally corresponded to our expectations in the sense that constructs and priorities that had emerged as central in the interview were evident in the teachers' instructional provisions, in the children's activities, and in the general functioning of the classroom. As far as we can judge, the interview and coding procedures tended to err in the direction of understatement—that is, in the direction of failure to elicit or detect significant features of constructs—rather than in the direction of overinterpretation.

In summary, the evidence indicates that an interview methodology such as the one reported here is a sensitive approach to the study of underlying constructs about teaching and learning that have visible counterparts in the classroom and that have a traceable continuity over time. This and other methodologies need to be refined for sustained and programmatic research on the origins, nature, and influence of teachers' thinking. Few areas of investigation are as important for understanding the educational process and few have been as seriously neglected. In speculating about the reasons for this neglect, we come full circle to concerns and questions raised at the beginning of the book.

> If the nature of man's everyday life experience is to be fathomed, it is necessary first of all to try to describe man's experience in appropriate terms. . . .
>
> By refusing to place firm reliance on variables that are labeled subjective, psychology has neglected some of the more important problems with which it should be concerned and has not done justice to the uniqueness of man.
>
> (Cantril, 1950, pp. 18-19)

Cantril's analysis of the situation is as contemporary today as it was over a quarter of a century ago when he wrote it. We believe, however, that psychological research over the next 25 years will

171

be more responsive. As Cantril goes on to say (p. 21), "the very complexity of the problems provides part of the motivation for trying to understand them."

REFERENCES

Allport, G. W. *Becoming: Basic considerations for a psychology of personality.* New Haven: Yale University Press, 1955.

Armington, D. E. *A plan for continuing growth.* Newton, Mass.: Education Development Center, 1968. Also in E. G. Nyquist and G. R. Hawes (eds.), *Open education: A source book for parents and teachers.* New York: Bantam Books, 1972. Pp. 63-72.

Bannister, D., and Fransella, F. *Inquiring man: The theory of personal constructs.* Baltimore: Penguin Books, 1971.

Beller, E. K. Research on organized programs of early education. In R. M. Travers (ed.), *Second handbook of research on teaching.* Chicago: Rand McNally, 1973.

Blackie, J. *Inside the primary school.* London: Her Brittanic Majesty's Stationery Office, 1967; New York: Schocken Books, 1971.

Buhler, C. Basic theoretical concepts of humanistic psychology. *American Psychologist,* 1971, *26*, 378-386.

Bussis, A. M., and Chittenden, E. A. *Analysis of an approach to open education* (PR-70-13). Princeton, N.J.: Educational Testing Service, 1970.

Cantril, H. *The "why" of man's experience.* New York: Macmillan, 1950.

Carini, P. F. *Observation and description: An alternative methodology for the investigation of human phenomena.* Grand Forks, N.D.: University of North Dakota, North Dakota Study Group on Evaluation, Center for Teaching and Learning, 1975.

Chein, I. *The science of behavior and the image of man.* New York: Basic Books, 1972.

Devaney, K. *Developing open education in America.* Washington, D.C.: National Association for the Education of Young Children, 1974.

Dewey, J. *Experience and education.* New York: Macmillan, 1938.

Dubos, R. The despairing optimist. *The American Scholar,* 1972, *41*, 508-512.

Duchastel, P., and Merrill, P. The effects of behavioral objectives on learning: A review of empirical studies. *Review of Educational Research,* 1973, *43*, 53-69.

Education Development Center. Conditions for growth. Unpublished working paper of Follow Through Program, Education Development Center, Newton, Mass., Spring 1972.

Eisner, E. Instructional and expressive educational objectives: Their formulation and use in curriculum. In *Instructional Objectives,* AERA Monograph Series on Curriculum, vol. 3. Chicago: Rand McNally, 1969.

Eisner, E. Emerging models for educational evaluation. *School Review,* 1971, *80*, 573-590.

Goodlad, J. Curriculum: State of the field. *Review of Educational Research,* 1969, *39*, 367-375.

Goodlad, J., Klein, M. F., and Associates. *Behind the classroom door.* Worthington, Ohio: Charles A. Jones Publishing Co., 1970.

Greene, M. *Teacher as stranger—Educational philosophy for the modern age.* Belmont, Calif.: Wadsworth Publishing Company, 1973.

Harvey, O. J., Hunt, D. E., and Schroder, H. M. *Conceptual systems and personality organization.* New York: Wiley, 1961.

Hawkins, D. Learning the unteachable. In L. Shulman and E. Keislar (eds.), *Learning by discovery: A critical appraisal.* Chicago: Rand McNally, 1966.

Hawkins, D. Informal talk presented at the Advisory for Open Education, Cambridge, Mass., October 1973.

Hawkins, D. *The informed vision: Essays on learning and human nature.* New York: Agathon Press, 1974. (See particularly "I, thou, and it," pp. 48-62, and "On understanding the understanding of children," pp. 195-206.)

Hawkins, F. P. *The logic of action.* New York: Pantheon Books, 1974.

Hazlewood, A. C., and Norris, M. A. *The open corridor program: An introduction for parents.* New York: City College of the City University of New York, Open Corridor Program, 1972. Also in E. G. Nyquist and G. R. Hawes (eds.), *Open education: A sourcebook for parents and teachers.* New York: Bantam Books, 1972.

Isaacs, S. *Childhood and after.* London: Routledge & Kegan Paul, 1948.

Isaacs, S. *The children we teach* (2nd ed., reset). London: Hodder and Stoughton, 1965.

Jackson, P. Is there a best way of teaching Harold Bateman? *Midway,* 1970, *10,* 15-28.

Jones, R. M. *Fantasy and feeling in education.* New York: New York University Press, 1968.

Katz, L. G. Some notes on the distinction between education and excitement. Unpublished paper, 1972.

Kelly, G. A. *The psychology of personal constructs,* vol. 1, *A theory of personality.* New York: W. W. Norton, 1955. (a)

Kelly, G. A. *The psychology of personal constructs,* vol. 2, *Clinical diagnosis and psychotherapy.* New York: W. W. Norton, 1955. (b)

Kelly, G. A. A brief introduction to personal construct theory. In D. Bannister (ed.), *Perspectives in personal construct theory.* New York: Academic Press, 1970.

Kliebard, H. The question in teacher education. In D. J. McCarty (ed.), *New perspectives on teacher education.* San Francisco: Jossey-Bass, 1973.

Langer, S. *Mind: An essay on human feeling,* vol. 1. Baltimore: The Johns Hopkins University Press, 1967.

Lenneberg, E. *Biological foundations of language.* New York: Wiley, 1967.

Lortie, D. C. The balance of control and autonomy in elementary school teaching. In A. Etzioni (ed.), *The semi-professions and their organization.* New York: Free Press, 1969. Pp. 1-53.

Macdonald, J. B. An evaluation of evaluation. *The Urban Review,* 1974, 7, 3-14.

Macdonald, J. B., and Clark, D. Critical value questions and the analysis of objectives and curriculum. In R. M. Travers (ed.), *Second handbook of research on teaching.* Chicago: Rand McNally, 1973.

Maslow, A. H. *Toward a psychology of being.* Princeton, N.J.: D. Van Nostrand, 1962.

May, R., Angel, E., and Ellenberger, H. (eds.). *Existence, a new dimension in psychiatry and psychology.* New York: Basic Books, 1958.

McPherson, G. H. *Small town teacher.* Cambridge: Harvard University Press, 1972.

Merleau-Ponty, M. *Sense and non-sense.* Evanston, Ill.: Northwestern University Press, 1964.

Nuthall, G., and Snook, I. Contemporary models of teaching. In R. M. Travers (ed.), *The second handbook of research on teaching.* Chicago: Rand McNally, 1973.

Piaget, J. *To understand is to invent.* New York: Grossman, 1973.

Piaget, J., and Inhelder, B. *The psychology of the child.* New York: Basic Books, 1969.

Polanyi, M. *Personal knowledge: Towards a post-critical philosophy.* Chicago: University of Chicago Press, 1958.

Polanyi, M. *Tacit dimension.* Garden City, N.Y.: Doubleday, 1966.

Popham, W. J. Curriculum materials. *Review of Educational Research,* 1969, *39,* 319-338.

Rogers, C. R. *Client-centered therapy: Its current practice, implications, and theory.* Boston: Houghton-Mifflin, 1951.

Rokeach, M. *Beliefs, attitudes, and values.* San Francisco: Jossey-Bass, 1970.

Sarason, S. B. *The culture of the school and the problem of change.* Boston: Allyn and Bacon, 1971.

Smith, F. *Understanding reading: A psycholinguistic analysis of reading and learning to read.* New York: Holt, Rinehart & Winston, 1971.

Smith, L. M., and Geoffrey, W. *Complexity of an urban classroom: An analysis toward a general theory of teaching.* New York: Holt, Rinehart & Winston, 1968.

Snygg, D., and Combs, A. *Individual behavior.* New York: Harper & Brothers, 1949.

Stephens, J. M. *The process of schooling.* New York: Holt, Rinehart & Winston, 1967.

Strike, K. E. On the expressive potential of behaviorist language. *American Educational Research Journal,* 1974, *11,* 103-120.

Thelen, H. A. Profession anyone? In D. J. McCarty (ed.), *New perspectives on teacher education.* San Francisco: Jossey-Bass, 1973.

Walker, D., and Schaffarzick, J. Comparing curricula. *Review of Educational Research,* 1974, *44,* 83-111.

Weber, L. *The English infant school and informal education.* Englewood Cliffs, N.J.: Prentice-Hall, 1971.

Zahorik, J. A. What good teaching is. *The Journal of Educational Research,* 1973, *66,* 435-440.

APPENDIXES

THE TEACHER INTERVIEW

PRELIMINARY QUESTIONS: BACKGROUND AND EXPERIENCE

a. How many years have you taught, including the current year? Has this teaching been continuous or interrupted?

b. How long have you taught in this school? In this school system?
     - comments on other schools in which you have taught?

c. What grade levels have you taught?

d. To what extent did your undergraduate college program focus on teacher education, e.g., education major, education minor in liberal arts program, little or no education courses?

e. Any course work at the graduate level?
     - towards degree?
     - extent and principal focus of the work?

f. Any other particular course of study or experiences that should be mentioned?

g. What grade level(s) are you presently teaching?
    - age range of children?

h. How many children are in your class?

i. Do you normally work with other children besides those in your class?
    - give details

j. How would you label the general physical setting in which you teach? Would you say it is primarily a self-contained classroom, primarily self-contained with considerable use of corridor or other shared space, or an open space setting?

k. Do you ordinarily work with another adult (teacher, aide, volunteer), or are you generally by yourself with the children? (No details here.)
    - Do you work less than half time or more than half time with another adult?

OVERALL VIEW OF TEACHING/LEARNING ACTIVITIES

1. Now, would you give a brief description of the organization of activities during the course of a typical school day? Starting with the time when the children arrive in the morning, what happens? (Answer in terms of present time.)

    Probe* for: - what are the specific things children typically do during any period the teacher has described as free choice or "project" time?

    - what is the teacher typically doing while children are working independently or in small groups?

    - are times for various activities fairly flexible or fixed?

    a. Are there things that children must do every day—or almost every day?

2. With children involved in different activities, on what basis do you divide your time and attention among them?

    Probe for: - is allocation of time and attention a problem for you?

    - has it ever been a problem?

---

*Probes are suggested in cases where the teacher's response does not produce enough information or where more in-depth questioning is indicated.

3. How much time do you spend outside of school hours on work connected with your teaching?

    a. Take last week as an example—what kinds of work connected with your teaching did you do outside of school hours?

Regarding planning time, probe as necessary:

> - what about planning and preparation time? Is this done during school or outside?
> - what were you planning or preparing?
> - how did you come to that decision? What made you decide to do _____?

PHYSICAL SETTING AND MATERIALS

4. What about the arrangement of the classroom—can you tell me how you have it set up generally?

    a. Has that been the general arrangement of the room all year?

> - what made you decide on this particular setup?
> - what prompted you to rearrange the room to this particular setup?
> - can you tell me how it got this way?

5. With respect to material resources—the things in your classroom—how did they come to be there? Who ordered them or brought them in?

    Probe for:
> - locus of decision (teacher, children, advisors, etc.)
> - leeway in decisions (ordering from prescribed list; any list)
> - homemade constructions (by teacher or by children)—what?
> - teacher buying things on own or bringing them from home—what? What prompted her to buy or bring material in?
> - children bringing things from home or neighborhood—what?

    a. Is there any particular material that you consider absolutely essential to your teaching? What? Why is it essential?

6. In your opinion, how valuable are the manufactured, semistructured kinds of material—things like Cuisenaire rods, puzzles, or balance scales? Why?

Probe for: - what type and variety of learning do they
promote as far as you have seen?
- any drawbacks or limitations?

7. What about natural and environmental materials—sand, water,
rocks, plants, tin cans, plastic bottles, egg cartons, and so on?
How valuable do you think this type of material is? Why?
Probe for: - kinds and variety of learning promoted
- any drawbacks or limitations?

8. If you had an extra sum of money in your teaching budget,
how would you use it?

CHILDREN IN THE CLASSROOM

9. In an open setting, children often work in small groups. What
benefits do you see in such small groupings?

10. Do you think that children tend to express their needs and feelings more freely in an open setting as compared with the more
conventional classroom?
a. Does this (i.e., relatively free expression of needs and feelings) pose any difficulties for a teacher? What?
b. Does it pose any difficulties for children? What?
c. What benefits do you see in a more open expression of
feelings?
d. What about sensitive content—such as sex, death, birth,
fears that children have? Do you think such content has
any place in the classroom? How would you use it?

11. You hear a lot about "building on children's interests" in an
open philosophy of education. But how does this work out in
practice? How do you go about utilizing or building on a
child's interests? Can you give me some concrete examples?
a. How about children who show little apparent interest in
anything that you have in the room, or who can't settle
down and get involved? How do you deal with that situation?

12. In most every class there are times when some child or a group
of children have a disruptive influence on the class. How do
you generally handle this kind of problem?

13. "Opening up" a classroom usually means giving children some amount of choice in what they do. In your experience, how do young children handle choice situations? Can they make choices? On what basis do they choose?

    Probe for:
    - do you think most choices reflect genuine interest, a passing whim, or what? How do you tell the difference?
    - perceived reason why some children can't handle choice very well or don't make purposeful choices (e.g., age, home background, personality problem, etc.)
    - how do you help children make choices— or can you?
    - does it bother you when a child persistently sticks to one or two activities?

14. Aside from making choices, what other kinds of responsibilities do children have to learn to assume in this type of program?

15. There appears to be a good deal of debate about this next question, and I'd like your reaction. Do you think an informal approach is suitable for all children?

    Probe for:
    - what children can't or don't benefit in an informal approach?
    - if an informal approach is suitable for all (or almost all)—why do you think so? How do you help children who may have initial difficulties?

EVALUATING TEACHING AND LEARNING

16. Of all the various goals you have in mind as a teacher, which one (or ones) do you think you've made pretty good progress toward accomplishing this year?

    Probe for:
    - what clues led the teacher to believe that progress has been made?

17. With what goal (or goals) do you feel least satisfied—least sure that you have accomplished much progress?

    Probe for:
    - what clues led the teacher to question whether much progress has been made?

18. In general, do you consider judging individual children's progress to be more or less difficult in an informal setting?

183

PERCEPTION OF TEACHING REQUIREMENTS AND REWARDS

19. What about your own interests—do you have any personal hobbies or interests that carry over to the classroom?

20. Do you think your own general knowledge in a subject area affects your capabilities or style as a teacher? In what ways?

    a.   Can an enthusiastic or accepting attitude toward a subject make up for lack of substantial knowledge in an area?

        Probe for: - can you give me an example from your own teaching of how:

                        enthusiasm carried you through?

                        enthusiasm wasn't enough?

    b.   If you had the opportunity to take an extended period of time off for learning, what would you want to learn about? How would you go about it?

21. To what degree do you think your actual physical presence is necessary to the smooth functioning of the class? For example, how do your children typically react to a substitute teacher?

        Probe for: - if they act badly, why?

22. Do you find that your teaching now, in this program, is more or less personally satisfying than your previous experience—or is it about the same?

            Probe for: - what are personal satisfactions?

                        - are there rewards in what the teacher is doing?

                        - or in what she observes children doing?

                        - or in some combination of both?

23. If another teacher who was going to start an open classroom came to you for advice, what are some tips or ideas that would come to mind to tell her?

WORKING ENVIRONMENT

THE ADVISORY

24. I'd like to ask you about _____ advisory. First of all, how did you come to be part of this program?
    Probe for: - locus of decision
                     - motivation (antecedents/"history")
                     - nature of any discontent

25. When you first began to work with _____, did you have a pretty good idea of what their approach was like?
    Probe for: - any initial skepticism
                     - any major turning points in understanding

26. What is the scope of the program—e.g., how many teachers are involved? How long has it been in existence at the school? Has there been any turnover of teachers?

27. Turning more to the advisory and its function, what are the ways you work with an advisor? What is the nature of the contact?
    Probe for: - after school meetings/workshops
                     - individual consultation
                     - advisors working with children/materials
                     - advisors observing

                     - do you usually initiate these contacts?
                     - are there ways of working with the advisors that you'd like to see happen more often?
    Clarify: - how many advisors do you work with?
                     - how frequently do you see them?

28. Have you attended any extended workshops during the past two years?
    Probe for: - how many?
                     - where? when?
                     - content of the workshop
                     - perceived benefits

29. In thinking about all the various aspects and functions of the advisory, what have you found particularly helpful?
    Probe for: - concrete examples (more than one)
                     - what is of perceived value to other teachers,

185

even though not directly helpful to you?
- any benefit carry over to school as a whole or community?

30. Are there some features that seem good but for one reason or another have not worked out as well as they might?

    Probe for: - suggestions for improvement and strengthening

31. Are there some ways that the advisory operates, or some of its policies that you have severe reservations about—that you feel definitely should be changed or abandoned?

    Probe for: - nature of the difficulty
                      - nature of change desired

32. If the advisory support and services were withdrawn—next year, say—what do you think would happen as far as your own teaching is concerned?

WORKSHOPS

[Alternate questions 24-32 used for teachers not connected with an advisory program.]

24. Before getting into this next section which concerns workshops —could you tell me first how you became interested in a more open or informal approach to teaching?

    Probe for: - motivation
                      - nature of discontent (if any)
                      - is anyone else at school working this way?

25. Give me a brief summary of your workshop experience.

    Probe for: - where; when; sponsorship

26. How is it that you first started going to the_____ workshop? Where did you hear about it and what prompted your interest?

    Probe for: - when did you start?
                      - how frequently do you attend workshops?
                      - who pays/under what auspices do you go?
                      - do others in the school attend_____ workshops?

27. Describe what you would consider a "typical" workshop. You go there and . . . what?

> Probe for:
> - what kinds of things is the teacher doing (constructing something; experimenting with materials; talking with staff; etc.)?
> - what is_____staff doing?
> - does the teacher make it a point to talk with staff about what she is doing or problems she may be having—or does staff do so?
> - is there extra-workshop help from staff (e.g., classroom visits)?

28. What do you see as the most important—the really crucial—components of a good workshop session(s), e.g., can be materials, equipment, staffing, group interactions, etc.?

> Probe for:
> - amount of direction from staff seen as desirable

29. What are the most important ways that your workshop activity has been useful to you? What is it you "get from" or "take from" the workshops?

> Probe for:
> - influence or effects in classroom

30. Are there some features of the_____workshops that you think should be changed or strengthened? Or perhaps something you have rather severe reservations about?

31. What about your future plans? Do you plan next year on going to_____ workshops?

> If yes:
> - any particular type of workshop sought
>
> If no:
> - reasons why not going back

a. Are there other forms of assistance for your teaching, in addition to workshops, that you would like to have?

32. (Depending on previous responses):

a. How would you contrast the operating philosophies or approaches of the different workshops you've attended?

> and/or

b. Thinking back, how do you see that your own needs are changing with respect to workshops?

> - Do you think this is a typical pattern of change for most teachers?

In the next questions, I'd like to get some idea of the ways in which you work with adults, other than advisors, in the school—such as other teachers, aides, parents, principal.

33. First, concerning teachers (not teachers designated as aides):

    Do teachers in your school work independently for the most part (with occasional staff meetings)—or do you work closely, team up with other teachers in some way?

    Probe for:
    - nature of cooperation (planning jointly, teaming, etc.)
    - extent of cooperation (pairs? larger groups? how much of the time?)
    - is attempt being made to extend interactions? or are they diminishing?

    a. What do you see as the benefits of working in this way? Any disadvantages?

    b. Do you have contact with teachers outside your immediate working group or outside of this school?

    Probe for:
    - do they help or support professional efforts, or are they purely social contacts?
    - where (school visits, teacher centers, etc.)?

34. Concerning the aide/paraprofessional working with you:

    a. What sorts of contributions does the aide make?

    b. What benefits or satisfactions does he/she receive?

    c. Do you see major differences between your role as the designated teacher and the role of the aide? What?

35. Turning now to the principal (vice-principal), what is the nature of your contact with him/her?

    Probe for:
    - forms of interactions (classroom visits, staff meetings, etc.)
    - extent of contact
    - typical content of interactions (education matters, policy matters, rules and regulations, etc.)

36. Concerning parents and the nature of your contact with them:

    a. Are there regular or routine times when you talk with parents about their children? When? Are these contacts very helpful as far as you are concerned?

b. Are there ways in which parents help in the classroom or contribute directly in other ways to your teaching?

Probe for: - concrete examples
                   - are these typical?

c. Do you think there has been any change in the nature of parent contact in the school since you've been in the program?

d. Do you think parents generally understand the goals you are trying to achieve in your teaching?

         - were there ever any difficulties on this score?
         - what do they seem to understand and what do they not understand?

THE SCHOOL AS AN INSTITUTION

37. Thinking now about the school as an institution, I'd like to ask about expectations regarding your responsibility for children. Are you considered responsible for teaching all aspects of the curriculum—or are there other teachers who instruct in certain special areas (music, art, etc.)?

         - Does another adult ever assume responsibility for instruction or supervision of the whole class?

a. On the whole, do you agree with this view of the teacher's responsibility for the curriculum?

b. Does the type of activity or atmosphere that occurs during these times generally fit in with your own program and goals for the children?

38. Are there any school policies, requirements, or regulations that interfere or conflict—in major ways—with your teaching?

Probe for: - what policies interfere
                   - the ways they interfere

a. Do you think there is anything you can do to influence a change in policy?

39. Are there any school policies you feel have been especially helpful or supportive of your efforts?

40. What do you see as the major concerns or preoccupations of the teaching staff at the present time (major issues of discussion or debate, at staff meetings or informally)?

Probe for: - have these changed over time?
              - since the program was initiated?

SUMMARY EVALUATION

41. Thinking back over all the people and resources that we have been talking about (the advisory, parents, aides, other teachers, principal), what or whom do you consider have been major sources of help and support in accomplishing your teaching objectives?

    Probe for: - do they still play this role in the teacher's life or has the support source been "outgrown?"

42. Looking back to your formal education, what do you think was the most valuable part of your educational training? What least valuable?

43. Looking ahead, where do you see yourself a few years from now?

CURRICULUM PRIORITIES CODING

The 17 curriculum priorities identified in the teacher interviews are presented below. The first 11 priorities are of a cognitive nature, whereas the last six have more of a personal/social emphasis. The letter in parentheses preceding each entry indicates whether the priority is considered a comprehensive priority (C), a middle-range priority (M-R), or a narrow priority (N). The column on the right-hand side shows the percentage of teachers who were coded for each priority. The table following the priority list shows the percentage distribution of teachers who were coded for two or more priorities (no teacher was coded for one priority only).

Curriculum Priorities	% Teachers Coded for Priority
	N = 60

(C) 1. *Reflectivity and Intention.* (If only one emphasis is present, circle to indicate which one.) Concern that children know "what they are about" and "why." Concern that children think through what they are doing, understand (in their own terms) what they are doing . . . interject their own purposes into an activity. 8

Curriculum Priorities	% Teachers Coded for Priority

(C) 2. *Construct/Discover/Pursue Interest.*   **13**
Concern that children sustain an involvement in meaningful activity (as defined from the child's perspective) that leads to new knowledge/insights/constructions.

(C) 3. *Cognitive Perspective.* Concern that   **8**
children encounter and come to value diverse areas of learning and the phenomena involved in them—e.g., music, art, literature, plant and animal life, ways of classifying and quantifying things.

(C) 4. *Proficiency/Competency Outcomes.*   **10**
Concern that children become versatile and proficient in one or more curricular content areas. Concern that the quality of work is high.

(C) 5. *Exchange/Share/Reciprocity.* Concern   **17**
with the reciprocity process in learning. Emphasis on children learning from each other (not just asking other children for answers). Active interchange of ideas, or group projects where each child contributes uniquely.

(M-R) 6. *Thinking/Solving.* Concern that children   **5**
learn how to solve problems and/or learn logical strategies. This may also take the form of an emphasis on children "thinking for themselves"—isolated from other concerns such as constructing, reflectivity, intentionality, etc.

(M-R) 7. *Deciding/Choosing.* Concern that children   **27**
contribute their ideas—their input—to the classroom. Concern that children become able to make choices, become independent decision-makers.

(M-R) 8. *Initiative/Independence.* Concern that   **32**
children begin to assume responsibility for their own learning—become self-directed in the sense that they need less guidance from the teacher.

Curriculum Priorities	% Teachers Coded for Priority

(M-R) 9. *Involvement/Doing.* Concern that children become engaged and involved in meaningful activity (as defined mainly from the teacher's perspective) that interests them.   57

(N) 10. *Busy/Doing.* Concern that children be occupied during the day—primarily a management concern.   7

(N) 11. *Grade-Level Facts and Skills.* Concern that children learn and be able to demonstrate knowledge of the required skills and basic facts expected of them at their particular grade level.   72

(C) 12. *Awareness and Acceptance of Self: Emotions/Abilities.* (If only one emphasis is present, circle to indicate which one.) Concern that children come to recognize and differentiate their feelings and abilities and accept them as legitimate and worthwhile. Knowing self and experiencing self-respect in order to cope better with life.   27

(C) 13. *Social Problem-solving/Appreciation of Others.* Concern with mutual respect/ sensitivity for others' feelings and ideas. Concern that children interact and negotiate so as to work through group and interpersonal problems.   37

(M-R) 14. *Self-expression.* Concern that children express themselves (feelings, opinions, etc.), but with little evidence that this expression is in the service of either personal or social growth (as in 12 and 13 above).   42

(M-R) 15. *Confidence/Contentment.* Concern that children feel good about themselves and their abilities . . . are happy and content in learning, and experience some sense of accomplishment. (This concern lacks the depth and richness of 12 above, as there is little evidence that the teacher has thought through the meaning of personal growth beyond a "happiness" notion.)   38

Curriculum Priorities	% Teachers Coded for Priority

(M-R) 16. *Personal/Social Responsibility.* Concern that children mature in direction of basic cultural expectations— take care of own needs and belongings, respect the property of others, learn to take turns, share, etc. This is a concern for basic socialization of the child.   **67**

(N) 17. *Good School Behavior/Docility.* Concern that children conform to a stereotypical pattern of school behavior—emphasis on politeness, working hard, settling down, not causing disruptions, etc. This is a concern for socialization into an adult stereotype, with little regard for the nature of children's internal experience.   **15**

Percentage Distribution of Number of Priorities Coded

Number of Priorities Coded	Percentage of Teachers N = 60
1	0
2	3
3	17
4	25
5	30
6	13
7	5
8	3
9	2
10	2
	100